BREAKING

BARRIERS

TEARING DOWN INVISIBLE BARRIERS

CHANGING YOUR SPEECH, SIGHT, HEARING AND THOUGHT FROM NEGATIVE TO POSITIVE

MATTHEW ASHIMOLOWO

© 2000 Matthew Ashimolowo

Published by Mattyson Media an imprint of MAMM
Matthew Ashimolowo Media Ministries
57 Waterden Road
Hackney Wick
London
E15 2EE

ISBN 1 874 646-36-8

Bible quotes are from the King James Bible
unless otherwise stated as the following:

Appreciation is expressed to the following publishers for sections of
translations reprinted:

The New Testament (Henry Alford)
The Epistles of Paul (W.J. Conybeare)
The New Testament in the translation of Monsignor Ronald Knox
The Centenary Translation: The New Testament in Modern English (Helen
Barrett Montgomery)
The New Testament in Modern English (J.B. Phillips)
The Twentieth Century New Testament
The Jerusalem Bible

P.16-20 and 36-44 quoted from "Keeping Your Dreams Alive"
© 1993 Matthew Ashimolow - Mattyson Media Company

Printed in England by Clays Ltd, St Ives plc

CONTENTS

INTRODUCTION

1. BREAKING THE SPEECH BARRIER.. 9

Why Break The Speech Barrier?................................... 14
Living By The Word.. 23
How To Tear The Barriers Down 26
Breaking The Speech Barrier - Through Prayer.............. 35
Breaking The Speech Barrier - Through Praise.............. 40

2. BREAKING THE SIGHT BARRIER 46

Why Break The Sight Barrier?.................................... 49
How To Break The Sight Barrier................................. 55
The Tools For Breaking Barriers................................. 63
Acquire and Pursue Vision.. 78
Keep An Unbroken Focus.. 96
Why Must You Focus?... 103
What To Focus On.. 106
How To Stay Focused... 108

3. BREAKING THE THOUGHT BARRIER 117

Barriers Of Unrewened Thought.................................. 120
The Process Of The Renewal Of The Mind.................... 125

4. BREAKING THE SOUND BARRIER 135

Hearing Problem.. 138
31 Ways To Break The Sound Barrier.......................... 144

5. THE BARRIER BREAKER ANOINTING 155

The Name Of Jesus... 156
The Anointing.. 157
The Blood Of Jesus... 159

INTRODUCTION

There was a great excitement when we moved into our new home, enough rooms, enough space and even extra. Just as we were moving in, noticing that there was enough space for cars in front of the house, the idea of converting the garage into an office hit me so hard. In a nutshell, interior designers were called in who did a make-to-fit furnishing for the place. To make it look nice on the inside, the old garage door had to be blocked from the inside, so that it was no longer a doorway for cars.

All entry into the garage is now through a side door which is smaller and just perfect, now that it is an office. Those who drive past our house or into our premises would see a garage and garage doors. The external door gives you the impression that you could just lift it and drive in. On the inside it has been bricked up and walled up.

There are four wonderful gifts which God has bestowed on mankind, two of them are most unique to Him. All four like the doors to my garage, were supposed to make things come into the garage, but having been bricked up, may stop things from entering. Man has been given the wonderful gifts of speech, sight, hearing and thinking.

Before we were born-again they were our only sources of receiving and processing information. You might simply say they were the gates to our total being - spirit, soul and body. From infancy until we come to Christ, we were trained a certain way to receive and process information using these four abilities.

Part of our training made us to exclude certain information, particularly that which did not fit into the natural way of looking at things. Anything which could not be seen, felt, touched, or tasted; anything which could not be repeated or seen with the natural eyes was said to be non-existent. We were therefore trained to stop certain things from coming into our lives.

Not only did we stop the things which we felt were unnatural, along the line we used these very senses to stop ourselves by developing habits and beliefs which were onerous to our own progress. Therefore through bad teaching and bad mentoring we allowed our ears to hear things that were not helpful. Our mouth spoke things that were not helpful to our lives and those around us. With our eyes we also focused on the things that were not helpful. This corrupted the fourth one, which is our thinking, so that our hearts became full of all kinds of wickedness both against ourselves and the people around us.

In the end what was meant to be the door to introduce us to favour, destiny, health, joy and peace, became the barrier to these things. It is my sincere desire that you will make the quality decision to turn things around and change your ear, mouth, thought and sight gates to a doorway and not a barrier. This will give you access to the fulfilment of your potential and your calling.

CHAPTER ONE

BREAKING THE SPEECH BARRIER

Children on a playground have learnt to handle verbal abuse from their friends or those with whom they fall out, with statements like 'sticks and stones may break my bones but words will not hurt me'. The content of that little rhyme is far from true. Words give life; words make people feel alive; words also bring death, destruction and disease. It all depends on the source from where it emanated.

God has put so much authority in words,

so that by the words of a man, he may either be justified or condemned. Jesus reiterated this truth in Matthew chapter 12:34-37:

O generation of vipers, how can ye, being evil, speak good things? for out of the abundance of the heart the mouth speaketh.
A good man out of the good treasure of the heart bringeth forth good things: and an evil man out of the evil treasure bringeth forth evil things.
But I say unto you, That every idle word that men shall speak, they shall give account thereof in the day of judgment.
For by thy words thou shalt be justified, and by thy words thou shalt be condemned.
Matthew 12:34-37 (KJV)

Solomon summarises emptiness or fullness as a by-product of the words of your mouth.

If you are blessed or lacking, your mouth had a lot to do with it.

Those who speak a curse into their life will fully reap the harvest of their confession, and the same goes for those who speak a blessing.

A man's belly shall be satisfied with the fruit of his mouth; and with the increase of his lips shall he be filled.
Death and life are in the power of the tongue: and they that love it shall eat the fruit thereof.
Proverbs 18:20-21 (KJV)

It is therefore important to know and understand at all times that

your words are either a blessing to you or a trap.

Thou art snared with the words of thy mouth, thou art taken with the words of thy mouth.
Proverbs 6:2 (KJV)

10

This in effect is a reason why the believer must learn to be silent when he has nothing to contribute to a matter, or is unsure. No one can quote or misquote your silence.

We have seen that blessings or curses come through words, so do health or disease. If a man will be healthy or sick, the words of his mouth will be a contributing factor.

Whoso loveth instruction loveth knowledge: but he that hateth reproof is brutish.
Proverbs 12:1 (KJV)

A man's word can also bring deliverance.

The words of the wicked are to lie in wait for blood: but the mouth of the upright shall deliver them.
Proverbs 12:6 (KJV)

The strength and power of words therefore means that you should choose who you would believe,

when a statement is made to you. For example if you go to your doctor and he tells you, you will die and not live, and you know that your life has not reached the fullness of the years promised the believer in Psalm 90:10.

The days of our years are threescore years and ten; and if by reason of strength they be fourscore years, yet is their strength labour and sorrow; for it is soon cut off, and we fly away.
Psalms 90:10 (KJV)

To break the speech barrier which has been placed upon you by that doctor, you must

learn to say what God says, "That you will live and not die".

One of the reasons you must learn to quickly reverse it and break that barrier is because words are also described as weapons, and you must stop the weapon of the enemy by rejecting the missile that has been sent to you.

No weapon that is formed against thee shall prosper; and every tongue that shall rise against thee in judgment thou shalt condemn. This is the heritage of the servants of the LORD, and their righteousness is of me, saith the LORD.
Isaiah 54:17 (KJV)

Speech barriers are created further when we allow the suggestions people make to us to stand without challenging it with God's Word.

Speech barriers remain in our lives when we believe an evil report above the Word which God Himself has spoken. A major barrier was put before Israel as they travelled from Egypt by the evil report of the ten spies who came back with a discouraging message.

Nevertheless the people be strong that dwell in the land, and the cities are walled, and very great: and moreover we saw the children of Anak there. The Amalekites dwell in the land of the south: and the Hittites, and the Jebusites, and the Amorites, dwell in the mountains: and the Canaanites

dwell by the sea, and by the coast of Jordan.
But the men that went up with him said, We be not able to go up against the people; for they are stronger than we.
And they brought up an evil report of the land which they had searched unto the children of Israel, saying, The land, through which we have gone to search it, is a land that eateth up the inhabitants thereof; and all the people that we saw in it are men of a great stature.
And there we saw the giants, the sons of Anak, which come of the giants: and we were in our own sight as grasshoppers, and so we were in their sight.
Numbers 13:28-29; 31-33 (KJV)

It is even safe to believe that the incident in Numbers 13 was a major reason why all of the adults, except Caleb and Joshua who left Egypt, never saw the Promised Land. The doors of the Promised Land were turned to a barrier, by both the evil report brought and their own inability to discern the Word of God from the lies of Satan.

Speech barriers are built when we allow close ones to say things and go free with it even where it is clearly not of God,

e.g. Peter to Jesus. Speech barriers are built when we sit in the wrong places, in the atmosphere where the Word and God are mocked.

Blessed is the man that walketh not in the counsel of the ungodly, nor standeth in the way of sinners, nor sitteth in the seat of the scornful.
Psalms 1:1 (KJV)

WHY BREAK THE SPEECH BARRIER?

It is important to know the reason for breaking the speech barrier, and I believe it begins with you understanding

that if you must experience God's miraculous power in your life, it begins with acting on His Word.

That simply is also what faith is, acting on God's Word.

And Simon answering said unto him, Master, we have toiled all the night, and have taken nothing: nevertheless at thy word I will let down the net.
Luke 5:5 (KJV)

You have to break that barrier because

as soon as the Word goes forth, you have to understand that the process has already started, even if there is no manifestation.

A person who consistently says "I think I'm gonna be sick" has put a process in motion, even if there is no manifestation yet. In the same vein is the person who says "I will not die but live to declare the glory of the Lord". Remember that when a film is exposed by the clicking of your taking a photograph, the process has begun, even though there is no manifestation of the image captured.

The words we speak are containers, they hold inside them what we enclose. They can convey power, faith, or fear. They can be

14

tools of abuse, or encouragement and blessing. Without touching a person; imagine yourself speaking to a friend or a close associate. If you told them 'please give me a cup of water' all you did was to send words, and a whole person stood up, took the cup of water and brought it to you. So what we say matters, the statement "words are cheap" is certainly far from true.

A lot of Christians are defeated most times in the area of their speech life. That is why just ten people misled a nation by misinforming them, and remember they were leaders of their various families.

My friend, it is time for you to enjoy the fruit of your lips. God does, you should, because God never expects anything without saying it first. He spoke the world into manifestation; He sends His Word and then heals the diseases of His people.

He sent his word, and healed them, and delivered them from their
destructions.
Psalms 107:20 (KJV)

When Jesus stood up in Capernaum to declare the mandate of His ministry, it was by the words of His mouth that He began to proclaim liberty to the captives, freedom to those who are oppressed.

The Spirit of the Lord is upon me, because he hath anointed me to preach the
gospel to the poor; he hath sent me to heal the brokenhearted, to preach
deliverance to the captives, and recovering of sight to the blind, to set at
liberty them that are bruised,
To preach the acceptable year of the Lord.
Luke 4:18-19 (KJV)

Therefore without the laying on of hands, He had set the deliverance of mankind in motion. Use your words to come out of every yoke of bondage.

Confession brings possession, you only get what you confess and believe in life.

The words you speak program your spirit for defeat or victory. So while others are looking and seeing difficulties, you are perpetually telling yourself what God is birthing in your spirit. Though surrounded by the majority, Joshua and Caleb saw possibilities and not obstacles, and in the face of the most towering opposition they still maintained their testimony.

And Caleb stilled the people before Moses, and said, Let us go up at once, and possess it; for we are well able to overcome it.
Numbers 13:30 (KJV)

And Joshua the son of Nun, and Caleb the son of Jephunneh, which were of them that searched the land, rent their clothes:
And they spake unto all the company of the children of Israel, saying, The land, which we passed through to search it, is an exceeding good land.
If the LORD delight in us, then he will bring us into this land, and give it us; a land which floweth with milk and honey.
Only rebel not ye against the LORD, neither fear ye the people of the land; for they are bread for us: their defence is departed from them, and the LORD is with us: fear them not.
Numbers 14:6-9 (KJV)

It is important though to understand that you must believe and say what you believe, and not just say what you have.

If you say what you have you would not increase. The words you speak will be the seed that goes into your future to be the harvest you would bring home. It is important to tear down the barriers because many times it is not the people we blame who stop us from possessing our possession; it is the words of our mouth.

Israel kept measuring the size of the giants in the land. The giants did not stop them, their self-talk did, because their self-talk determined their self-value.

And there we saw the giants, the sons of Anak, which come of the giants: and we were in our own sight as grasshoppers, and so we were in their sight.
Numbers 13:33 (KJV)

In the valley of Elah, We observe that Goliath came out roaring everyday, it was not his size, spear, sword or shield that stopped Israel though. It was their belief and self-talk, because the giant outside could become a gargantuan inside by reason of a person's confession. Storms and giants only assume the power and capability we give to them. If you raise the Word of God above a storm, that thing becomes subject to God's Word. There is no special problem in life; there is no special mountain. If it seems so, you specialised it!

If the barriers erected by your speech must come down at all, one key reason must be because the person most affected by whatever you say is you. The human body is intricately designed in such a way that the part of the brain which connects to our speech also has direct and indirect connections to the whole of our body. The implication of that is, if you declare health to your body, it is sent to every nook and cranny of your total makeup.

It is most interesting to also discover that you have an inner ear, it seems to me that that was so designed by God, so that while you hear externally, your inner man can also hear what you are saying to yourself. This makes it important for you to watch what you say, more than what anyone else's words say. So if a person calls you a thief, you only register probably with the ear. But if you say to yourself "I am blessed", your ears hear it and your speech skills carry it to every nook and cranny of your body.

God created the world by the words of His mouth; we are also told He sustains it by the Word of His power. So without the Word of God, "there was nothing made that was made".

In the beginning was the Word, and the Word was with God,
and the Word was God.
The same was in the beginning with God.
All things were made by him; and without him was not any thing made that
was made.
John 1:1-3 (KJV)

If anything must shape the image and picture of how you should view life, the world and your destiny, it must be the Word of God.

He framed the universe with the Word.

> *Through faith we understand that the worlds were framed by the word of God, so that things which are seen were not made of things which do appear.*
> *Hebrews 11:3 (KJV)*

If you allow the enemy, he also wants to put an image in you, but that image will destroy what God has planned to give you. On the other hand when you say what God says, you will end up with what God has planned, and with the reality of God's Word being manifest in you and through you.

Speaking God's Word will fill you with faith, because it is already loaded with faith.

It is not ordinary words, Jesus said "The words that I speak are spirit and life". Learn the power of the spoken word. This is where the believer must learn to operate like Jesus did. It is not enough to learn about the Word, or be an ardent Bible student, it is important to reach the highest point of God's Word, which is the spoken Word. So as you speak forth the Word, it transmits faith for action, just as speaking negative words transmit fear. It is important to speak the Word of God, as it relates to life not death.

It is the spirit that quickeneth; the flesh profiteth nothing: the words that I
speak unto you, they are spirit, and they are life.
John 6:63 (KJV)

Call the things that be-not as though they were.

Because it is in the 'calling' that the manifestation finds its birthing.

(As it is written, I have made thee a father of many nations,) before him
whom he believed, even God, who quickeneth the dead, and calleth those
things which be not as though they were.
Romans 4:17 (KJV)

As you develop the habit of speaking the Word of God, do it prophetically by declaring how the end will be from the beginning of it.

They shall not hunger nor thirst; neither shall the heat nor sun smite them:
for he that hath mercy on them shall lead them, even by the springs of water
shall he guide them.
Isaiah 49:10 (KJV)

Learn to make your prayer correspond with your confession.

To pray a different way as if begging and to quote the scriptures authoritatively as if speaking the Word of faith, is to speak with 'two sides of the mouth'. Let your prayer and your confession be birthed in the womb of faith.

Learn to declare new things to your life.

See how former predictions have come true./ Fresh things I now fortell;/ before they appear I tell you of them.
Isaiah 42:9 (Jerusalem Bible).

Always remember that Jesus said He gave you the power,

And I will give unto thee the keys of the kingdom of heaven: and whatsoever thou shalt bind on earth shall be bound in heaven: and whatsoever thou shalt loose on earth shall be loosed in heaven.
Matthew 16:19 (KJV)

Verily I say unto you, Whatsoever ye shall bind on earth shall be bound in heaven: and whatsoever ye shall loose on earth shall be loosed in heaven.
Matthew 18:18 (KJV)

As you come into the realisation that there is power in the words which you speak, you must

ask the Lord to sanctify your lips, so that everything you say will be taken seriously by you and God.

But unto the wicked God saith, What hast thou to do to declare my statutes, or that thou shouldest take my covenant in thy mouth?
Psalms 50:16 (KJV)

After all, suppose everything you say comes to pass, would your house not be filled with all manner of things you really never needed? That is why you need the Lord to deal with your mouth, so that you only say what He says.

To whom shall I speak, and give warning, that they may hear? behold, their ear is uncircumcised, and they cannot hearken: behold, the word of the LORD is unto them a reproach; they have no delight in it.
Jeremiah 6:10 (KJV)

LIVING BY THE WORD

In order to give power to the content of your word, since anointing is dissipated in words; healing is conveyed in words; deliverance, salvation, favour and blessing are conveyed in words. Learn to live by the authoritative and creative Word of God, so that when you open your mouth and speak, it carries God's authoritative power and brings hope to the hopeless. Rise above evil by the power of the spoken Word, so that when a curse is pronounced against you, or an evil is sent, you boldly declare that it will not work. As you live in victory and confess it daily, apparent defeat will have to depart because you have chosen not to acknowledge its presence.

Applying God's Word to every situation reverses what would have happened in the negative.

Wrong application means an exposure to defeat. Walk in the reality of the fact that every principle in the Bible is there for your benefit and therefore train yourself to speak it, believe it, act it out, just as it was said. When you do that you release God's ability through the Word which you speak.

If God's Word says healing, do not debate it, do not question the time, and do not imagine it has gone past its sell by date.

Every Word of God is effective and profitable.

All scripture is given by inspiration of God, and is profitable for doctrine,
for reproof, for correction, for instruction in righteousness:
2 Timothy 3:16 (KJV)

If Jesus said it, take it personally, act it out, speak it out without a shadow of a doubt.

For verily I say unto you, That whosoever shall say unto this mountain, Be
thou removed, and be thou cast into the sea; and shall not doubt in his heart,
but shall believe that those things which he saith shall come to pass; he shall
have whatsoever he saith.
Therefore I say unto you, What things soever ye desire, when ye pray,
believe that ye receive them, and ye shall have them.
Mark 11:23-24 (KJV)

God never does anything without saying it first.

Have you noticed how every major step you have taken, you spoke it first? You told someone. Do not wait for it to be a major decision, begin to speak the Word of God first, and then act it out! As you do so a spiritual force is released by the content of the word that comes from your mouth, becoming a conduit of God's Word. The same Word that flows through you goes to perform and never comes back to the One who sent it void.

So shall my word be that goeth forth out of my mouth: it shall not return unto me void, but it shall accomplish that which I please, and it shall prosper in the thing whereto I sent it.
Isaiah 55:11 (KJV)

If it has not manifested, keep muttering the Word and meditating on it.

Continuous meditation on what you have based your prayer on strengthens your faith in the days of your expectation of a result.

This book of the law shall not depart out of thy mouth; but thou shalt meditate therein day and night, that thou mayest observe to do according to all that is written therein: for then thou shalt make thy way prosperous, and then thou shalt have good success.
Joshua 1:8 (KJV)

If you see somebody else doing or saying something contrary to your confession, do not do it! That may be what God told him to do, or he may be acting out of flesh in unbelief. Your report is the Word of the Lord, and it is only when you act on God's Word that His creative ability will be released, not when you act on the suggestions of people.

HOW TO TEAR THE BARRIERS DOWN

You must understand that ancient landmarks are not easy to tear down. Habits formed over a long period of time want to linger, but by standing on God's Word, your victory will become manifest.

Start with re-training yourself to study the Word of God at your level.

For every one that useth milk is unskilful in the word of righteousness: for he is a babe.
But strong meat belongeth to them that are of full age, even those who by reason of use have their senses exercised to discern both good and evil.
Hebrews 5:13-14 (KJV)

As you do that,

let the Word of God develop the God-kind of faith in you.

Faith is what gives you access into the blessings of the Lord.

But without faith it is impossible to please him: for he that cometh to God must believe that he is, and that he is a rewarder of them that diligently seek him.
Hebrews 11:6 (KJV)

Let the Word of God influence your prayer, so that you begin to declare what God says and decree what God's

intention is concerning a situation you are facing.

Thou shalt also decree a thing, and it shall be established unto thee: and the light shall shine upon thy ways.
Job 22:28 (KJV)

God gave you permission to decree a thing, in other words He wants you to imitate Him.

To imitate a person you must talk and act like he would do. Always remember whom God says you are when you are making these confessions or else the enemy will take advantage and accuse you of arrogance or bragging.

For thou hast possessed my reins: thou hast covered me in my mother's womb.
I will praise thee; for I am fearfully and wonderfully made: marvellous are thy works; and that my soul knoweth right well.
My substance was not hid from thee, when I was made in secret, and curiously wrought in the lowest parts of the earth.
Thine eyes did see my substance, yet being unperfect; and in thy book all my members were written, which in continuance were fashioned, when as yet there was none of them.
Psalms 139:13-16 (KJV)

Do not keep what you believe inside you, say it out for the world to know where you stand.

Erase idle words with your new confession of faith.

For verily I say unto you, That whosoever shall say unto this mountain, Be thou removed, and be thou cast into the sea; and shall not doubt in his heart, but shall believe that those things which he saith shall come to pass; he shall have whatsoever he saith.
Mark 11:23 (KJV)

So then faith cometh by hearing, and hearing by the word of God.
Romans 10:17 (KJV)

O generation of vipers, how can ye, being evil, speak good things? for out of the abundance of the heart the mouth speaketh.
Matthew 12:34 (KJV)

As you speak the Word of God, let it help you to release what your desire is, let it help you to release what your destiny will be. Use the Word to establish the vision God has placed on your heart. Write the words, but also speak it. Let your vision speak through you. Use the word in your mouth now to command.

Thus saith the LORD, the Holy One of Israel, and his Maker, Ask me of things to come concerning my sons, and concerning the work of my hands command ye me.
Isaiah 45:11 (KJV)

Let the words of your mouth confirm what God has promised in your heart. Always remember that the confession must precede the manifestation. As soon as the photograph is taken the process has begun. Use that Word to bring healing.

He sent his word, and healed them, and delivered them from their destructions.
Psalms 107:20 (KJV)

Use your word to express faith.

So then faith cometh by hearing, and hearing by the word of God.
Romans 10:17 (KJV)

Sow the seed of your expectation by reason of the confession of your mouth.

And he said, So is the kingdom of God, as if a man should cast seed into the ground;
And should sleep, and rise night and day, and the seed should spring and grow up, he knoweth not how.
Mark 4:26-27 (KJV)

Use your confession to renew your mind, say whom God says you are, your inner ears are passing it on to the whole of your body.

And be not conformed to this world: but be ye transformed by the renewing of your mind, that ye may prove what is that good, and acceptable, and perfect, will of God.
Romans 12:2 (KJV)

Use the Word to keep your answers before you.

Let it constantly remind you of what God has already put in motion for you.

Be careful for nothing; but in every thing by prayer and supplication with thanksgiving let your requests be made known unto God.
And the peace of God, which passeth all understanding, shall keep your hearts and minds through Christ Jesus.
Finally, brethren, whatsoever things are true, whatsoever things are honest, whatsoever things are just, whatsoever things are pure, whatsoever things are lovely, whatsoever things are of good report; if there be any virtue, and if there be any praise, think on these things.
Philippians 4:6-8 (KJV)

Let the Word challenge your heart to change, let it influence what flows out of your heart.

My son, attend to my words; incline thine ear unto my sayings.
Let them not depart from thine eyes; keep them in the midst of thine heart.
For they are life unto those that find them, and health to all their flesh.
Keep thy heart with all diligence; for out of it are the issues of life.
Proverbs 4:20-23 (KJV)

Let the Word of God confirm the confidence you have in God.

And whatsoever we ask, we receive of him, because we keep his commandments, and do those things that are pleasing in his sight.
1 John 3:22 (KJV)

Make your tongue the pen that will write your healing and favour.

Make your tongue the pen that will write your new vision and desire.

My heart is inditing a good matter: I speak of the things which I have made touching the king: my tongue is the pen of a ready writer.
Psalms 45:1 (KJV)

Love the Word more than your necessary food.

Address every situation and even the devil by saying what God says, and not what he wants you to say.

But he answered and said, It is written, Man shall not live by bread alone, but by every word that proceedeth out of the mouth of God.
Jesus said unto him, It is written again, Thou shalt not tempt the Lord thy God.
Then saith Jesus unto him, Get thee hence, Satan: for it is written, Thou shalt worship the Lord thy God, and him only shalt thou serve.
Matthew 4:4, 7, 10 (KJV)

Keep sowing the seed of the Word of God for the situation and the thing you are facing, even if there is no manifestation yet.

A delayed harvest is better than no harvest. If you do not sow, you will not reap; but watch what you sow. If you sow love, you reap love; a person who sows strife, will reap a harvest of strife. The seed you sow only multiplies back to you.

Sow the seed of the Word as it relates to the vision in your heart. As you do this you break the barriers which have been in place for a long time.

The fact that you saw lack and problems does not mean that you should make that your focus.

Speak the abundance and peace of God. A seed will not produce until you plant it. The ability to speak God's Word consistently will re-train your mind not pray the problem, but the solution. Praying the problem destroys your faith, whereas the Word of God builds it up. And when you face a mountain, you do not get help if you describe the mountain. Speak your intentions to the mountain like Zerrubabel did.

For verily I say unto you, That whosoever shall say unto this mountain, Be thou removed, and be thou cast into the sea; and shall not doubt in his heart, but shall believe that those things which he saith shall come to pass; he shall have whatsoever he saith.
Mark 11:23 (KJV)

Who art thou, O great mountain? before Zerubbabel thou shalt become a plain: and he shall bring forth the headstone thereof with shoutings, crying, Grace, grace unto it.
Zechariah 4:7 (KJV)

Resign from the group of complainers and critics.

Neither filthiness, nor foolish talking, nor jesting, which are not convenient: but rather giving of thanks.
Ephesians 5:4 (KJV)

Welcome yourself to the company of those who live and enjoy the comfort of God.

A man hath joy by the answer of his mouth: and a word spoken in due season, how good is it!
Proverbs 15:23 (KJV)

As you do this your faith will climb and you will be able to talk yourself out of problem into opportunities; out of obstacles into miracles. You will be able to change your barriers into your doors.

Breaking barriers is acting like Jesus would do in the same situation.

He called water wine, He declared the final intention.

And he saith unto them, Draw out now, and bear unto the governor of the feast. And they bare it.
John 2:8 (KJV)

33

He called the crooked to become straight.

And he laid his hands on her: and immediately she was made straight, and glorified God.
Luke 13:13 (KJV)

He called a man who was dead, living and the man came alive.

And said, Where have ye laid him? They said unto him, Lord, come and see.
John 11:34 (KJV)

In a storm He said peace, and His intention was established.

And the same day, when the even was come, he saith unto them, Let us pass over unto the other side.
Mark 4:35 (KJV)

The leprous He called clean, and their skin obeyed the words of His authority.

BREAKING THE SPEECH BARRIER - THROUGH PRAYER

The believer in the third millennium is confronted with realities beyond the imaginations and thoughts of Christians who lived several hundreds of years ago.

We are the generation confronted with increasing problems in the spiritual, religious, economic, political and social arenas.

This is also a time of great privilege. We are possibly the ones given the opportunity to prepare for the second advent of our Lord and Saviour, Jesus Christ. This challenging time on earth, the brevity of the day of man and the urgency of God's appearance makes the importance of prayer a matter of strong conviction.

Prayer is the staff the Christian pilgrim leans upon as he walks with God.

Prayer is the believer's opportunity to verbalize the needs of his heart. It is the breath of our spirit. Food is necessary for the body. Socialisation is necessary for the mind. Prayer - like the Word of God - is necessary for the nourishment of our spirit. It is God's great conveyor belt, bringing blessings and showers of blessings from above.

We need to pray.

Prayer is important because it is our opportunity to turn the desires of our hearts - the visions and dreams of our lives - to a God-ward motion.

It brings us into fellowship with the Father, so that we are truly able to cry to Him "Abba Father."

Prayer is a mine, full of rich supernatural minerals waiting to be brought out. It is the only way for the believer to reach God's great favour and blessing, and to partner with God to do divine exploits on earth. The world is waiting for a change. We must not surrender the fight to pray, for in doing so we would suspend all advancement for the kingdom and ourselves. Prayerlessness is the very thing that prepares the world for the anti-Christ to take over.

The church is supposed to be the voice of Jesus, resounding upon the earth and doing great exploits for Him.

We are not supposed to resign while we wait for His coming. We are supposed to occupy until He comes, and prayer is our greatest tool for obtaining dominion in this world as we look for Christ's return.

Prayer is touching heaven and causing heaven to touch earth.

Prayer is the one thing that can touch the One whose hands hold the whole world. Yes, He has the whole world in His hands, but His hands are not stiff that they cannot be moved. He's not so busy that He cannot hear us.

Prayer becomes the believer's staff to keep us from falling in a world of darkness.

It is the believer's battle-axe in the arena of warfare so that we do not lose. It is our awesome spear to bring down the enemy who has risen against us. Prayer helps us to prevail with God, so that when we would have accepted a "no," we keep holding on until the change comes.

Prayer tells us also to prevail against our arch enemy, Satan.

In spite of all his wiles, his strategies and tactics with the governments of his kingdom (which are principalities, powers, rulers and spirits of darkness), we still are able to overcome. The youngest, humblest, simplest believer on his knees can shake the whole of Satan's kingdom when he breaks forth with the Name of Jesus in prayer.

More prayer, more answers; less prayer, less answers.

Prayer helps us to prevail against Satan, so we must pray. It is the key to peace. A baby bird in a ruffled forest can find solace under its mother's wings because the care is not its own, but the mother's. Prayer helps us to cast our burden upon the Lord and find our peace and calmness in a world of trouble. It gives us boldness to stand before the One who says, *"Come that you may find help."* *(Hebrews 4:16)*

Prayer is our future; no prayer, no future.

Prayer helps us to properly occupy our place: *"You are a chosen generation, a royal priesthood..."* *(1 Peter 2:9)* Prayer is important indeed to our Christian life; it is the shedding of a tear not going unnoticed. Prayer is the upward glance of an eye to the Father, being able to call out to the one who made us. Children can do it; they can spell out their need in A-B-C. It is the breath of the soul so that our spirits are kept alive, even in a dying world.

Prayer is our last word before we pass over.

Jesus said *"Father forgive them for they know not what they are doing."* *(Luke 23:34)* Jesus said, *"Father into Thy hand have I committed my spirit."* *(Luke 23:46)* Prayer gives you resounding victory under the new covenant, so that when we lift up our voices and breathe His holy Name in prayer, heaven moves, angels are on assignment, things begin to happen because somebody decided to knock on the door of heaven with the one thing the Father gave us.

Do not do it when all else fails; do it all the time. Paul said, *"pray without ceasing." (I Thessalonians 5:17)* A corrupt heart, a busy devil and a wicked world makes prayer mandatory. Do not stop praying - that is where your victory lies.

BREAKING THE SPEECH BARRIER - THROUGH PRAISE

The next tool with which you can break the speech barrier is to learn to constantly praise the Lord, even when you are surrounded by junk, turn it to the tool which you use to praise God.

Praise is your responsibility which you cannot pass to somebody else,

it is your weapon with which to go to war against the wiles of the enemy. It is the tool to dig you out of the dungeon of trouble when it seems like you would not be able to come out.

Those who have learned to exalt God end up exalted themselves.

The LORD taketh pleasure in them that fear him, in those that hope in his mercy.
Psalms 147:11 (KJV)

I will extol thee, O LORD; for thou hast lifted me up, and hast not made my foes to rejoice over me.
Psalms 30:1 (KJV)

Praise is what makes your case clear to God and prepares you for His divine vindication.

The voice of thanksgiving must not be reduced in your house because it will produce multiplication.

And Jesus took the loaves; and when he had given thanks, he distributed to the disciples, and the disciples to them that were set down; and likewise of the fishes as much as they would.
John 6:11 (KJV)

Those who have learnt to praise God would discover that

it is the instrument by which He changes your position and lifts you to a new realm of favour.

And being not weak in faith, he considered not his own body now dead, when he was about an hundred years old, neither yet the deadness of Sara's womb:
He staggered not at the promise of God through unbelief; but was strong in faith, giving glory to God;
Romans 4:19-20 (KJV)

If you honour God you will be honoured too.

Honour the LORD with thy substance, and with the firstfruits of all thine increase:
Proverbs 3:9 (KJV)

Tear down the barriers which your tongue may want to bring.

Make praise your native language and you would rise and live in the presence of God. Make praise your native language and you will be understood in the throne room of heaven.

So no matter who wants to stop you, praise is the instrument by which you can break free from their attempt to control you.

The God you serve inhabits praise not problems, He does not sit in the midst of trouble or complaints and if you must get His attention remove the barrier of complaining, mumuring and arguing. Start using your tongue to worship God. Your day of victory will begin to manifest.

We go through period of nights and dark times seem not to change. But if you must come out of your night differently, if you must come out of your dark days, start praising Him. Praise is a seed and when it is sown, the harvest which follows is the abundance of God's peace.

But the meek shall inherit the earth; and shall delight themselves in the abundance of peace.
Psalms 37:11 (KJV)

Heaven's gate obeys the voice of praise and thanksgiving.

And at midnight Paul and Silas prayed, and sang praises unto God: and the prisoners heard them.
And suddenly there was a great earthquake, so that the foundations of the prison were shaken: and immediately all the doors were opened, and every one's bands were loosed.
Acts 16:25-26 (KJV)

If you must break out from the prisons of man or devils start to worship and praise God.

O let not the oppressed return ashamed: let the poor and needy praise thy name.
Psalms 74:21 (KJV)

Bring my soul out of prison, that I may praise thy name: the righteous shall compass me about; for thou shalt deal bountifully with me.
Psalms 142:7 (KJV)

Job confronted with the roughest of problems declared with boldness, "Though He slay me, I will yet praise Him". Whatever barriers have tried to stop you before, it is time to make yourself unstoppable and cause your destiny to be manifest by thanksgiving.

Now thanks be unto God, which always causeth us to triumph in Christ, and maketh manifest the savour of his knowledge by us in every place.
2 Corinthians 2:14 (KJV)

43

Those who have learned to give God worship and praise have also signified that they know who is in charge.

By thee have I been holden up from the womb: thou art he that took me out of my mother's bowels: my praise shall be continually of thee.
Psalms 71:6 (KJV)

The believer's invincible weapon which he can use his speech for is thanksgiving and praise.

And when they began to sing and to praise, the LORD set ambushments against the children of Ammon, Moab, and mount Seir, which were come against Judah; and they were smitten.
2 Chronicles 20:22 (KJV)

Make your praise stop Satan dead in his tracks.

In every thing give thanks: for this is the will of God in Christ Jesus concerning you.
1 Thessalonians 5:18 (KJV)

Qualitative breakthrough is a product of great praise.

So they came up to Baalperazim; and David smote them there. Then David said, God hath broken in upon mine enemies by mine hand like the breaking forth of waters: therefore they called the name of that place Baalperazim.
1 Chronicles 14:11 (KJV)

Are you facing dead situations that have been caused by your previous confession? Have barriers been erected to stop you from reaching your destiny? It is not time to count the problems but give thanks in advance before there is a manifestation.

(As it is written, I have made thee a father of many nations,) before him whom he believed, even God, who quickeneth the dead, and calleth those things which be not as though they were.
He staggered not at the promise of God through unbelief; but was strong in faith, giving glory to God;
Romans 4:17, 20 (KJV)

Every barrier must fall,

every Satanic spirit that has risen against you must be silenced, but you achieve this by praise.

Let the high praises of God be in their mouth, and a twoedged sword in their hand;
To execute vengeance upon the heathen, and punishments upon the people;
To bind their kings with chains, and their nobles with fetters of iron;
Psalm 149:6-8 (KJV)

CHAPTER TWO

BREAKING THE SIGHT BARRIER

One of the senses which make man to be able to make sense of his environment is sight. Its use has been responsible for the popular acronym "wy-si-wyg". **What you see is what you get.** Whether that is true or not is the purpose of our exposition in this chapter. The natural man depends on his physical sight to make sense of things, direction, his environment, relationships, and what eventually he desires.

Matter-of-fact other statements which make the physical sight primary, have been developed over the years. Statements like "seeing is believing". In the light of this statement and many others man has allowed his eyes to guide him in making decisions that are major and minor.

A search in scripture makes us to see that the natural sight, while great and important for direction, is not what should be depended on totally for making the decisions that affect our spiritual, mental, physical and emotional life.

There is another sight which is spiritual sight or inner sight. Your immediate physical sight can become a barrier to your future, but the application of the Word of God and the development of your inner sight helps you to go further than the natural sight would have allowed.

One of the scriptures which come immediately headlong against this view point is 2 Corinthians 4:18:

While we look not at the things which are seen, but at the things which are not seen: for the things which are seen are temporal; but the things which are not seen are eternal.
2 Corinthians 4:18 (KJV)

Meanwhile I look not to things seen, but to things unseen - for the things that are seen pass away, but the things that are unseen endure for ever.
2 Corinthians 4:18 (Con)

If only we will fix our eyes on what is unseen, not on what we can see - What we can see, lasts but for a moment..
2 Corinthians 4:18 (Knox)

...the visible things are transitory: it is the invisible things that are really permanent.
2 Corinthians 4:18b (Phillips)

....for what is seen is transient, but what is unseen is imperishable
2 Corinthians 4:18b (TCNT)

....for the things which are seen are for a time.....
2 Corinthians 4:18b (Alf)

These various renderings by the translations quoted make it clear, that our focus should not be on the temporary and the seen. At the same time, the scripture verse sounds like a contradiction. If we are not to look at the things that are seen, how can we see the things that are unseen. The verse assumes that the believer understands that he has spiritual eyes with which to look and to judge things and therefore impose upon the natural what he sees in the spirit realm.

A focus on the natural is dangerous because the natural sight tends to influence faith in a negative way,

making you to begin to disbelieve because of the enormity of the problem you see. Israel was captivated by Goliath's size because they looked at his natural person, while David came and saw Goliath from a spiritual point of view. Lot focused on the natural things that could be found in Sodom and Gomorrah, the lushness of the grass and vegetation. The natural overruled his ability to discern spiritually.

If you focus on the external, it begins to determine how you move and walk,

and the enemy of your progress even the devil, therefore uses what should have been the doorway to be a barrier and his access to stealing what belongs to you.

The thief cometh not, but for to steal, and to kill, and to destroy:
John 10:10 (KJV)

48

WHY BREAK THE SIGHT BARRIER?

It is possible that up until the time you started reading this book, your natural sight has guided your decision. You probably chose your marriage partner, purely because of what he or she looked like. We know that is misleading because the scripture says beauty is nothing.

Favour is deceitful, and beauty is vain: but a woman that feareth the LORD, she shall be praised.
Proverbs 31:30 (KJV)

You need to break the sight barrier because what you see shapes what you get.

If you focus on sickness, because that is all you see, you get sickness permanently. If you focus on problems that are called temporary, they begin to shape your belief, what you desire and how you conduct your life. It is important to recognise that a man cannot rise beyond what he sees.

For our light affliction, which is but for a moment, worketh for us a far more exceeding and eternal weight of glory;
2 Corinthians 4:17 (KJV)

Joseph saw himself one day in the palace, making decisions that affect many peoples destiny. That was what he became because he held on to what his inner sight showed him. Elijah acted on what he saw when he had the benefit and opportunity to poke into the spirit realm and see the rain before there was any cloud in the sky.

Divine insight helps you to live above the natural realm to see the things God sets in motion to do.

Insight gives you opportunity to be able to break the barriers and receive what God has already put there. Two men living together, Gehazi and Elisha.

Elisha allowed the eye of the spirit to guide his decisions; he was able to walk away from the niceties which Naaman brought.

Now Naaman, captain of the host of the king of Syria, was a great man with his master, and honourable, because by him the LORD had given deliverance unto Syria: he was also a mighty man in valour, but he was a leper.
And the Syrians had gone out by companies, and had brought away captive out of the land of Israel a little maid; and she waited on Naaman's wife.
And she said unto her mistress, Would God my lord were with the prophet that is in Samaria! for he would recover him of his leprosy.
And one went in, and told his lord, saying, Thus and thus said the maid that is of the land of Israel.
And the king of Syria said, Go to, go, and I will send a letter unto the king of Israel. And he departed, and took with him ten talents of silver, and six thousand pieces of gold, and ten changes of raiment.
And he brought the letter to the king of Israel, saying, Now when this letter is come unto thee, behold, I have therewith sent Naaman my servant to thee, that thou mayest recover him of his leprosy.
And it came to pass, when the king of Israel had read the letter, that he rent

his clothes, and said, Am I God, to kill and to make alive, that this man doth send unto me to recover a man of his leprosy? wherefore consider, I pray you, and see how he seeketh a quarrel against me.

And it was so, when Elisha the man of God had heard that the king of Israel had rent his clothes, that he sent to the king, saying, Wherefore hast thou rent thy clothes? let him come now to me, and he shall know that there is a prophet in Israel.

So Naaman came with his horses and with his chariot, and stood at the door of the house of Elisha.

And Elisha sent a messenger unto him, saying, Go and wash in Jordan seven times, and thy flesh shall come again to thee, and thou shalt be clean.

But Naaman was wroth, and went away, and said, Behold, I thought, He will surely come out to me, and stand, and call on the name of the LORD his God, and strike his hand over the place, and recover the leper.

Are not Abana and Pharpar, rivers of Damascus, better than all the waters of Israel? may I not wash in them, and be clean? So he turned and went away in a rage.

And his servants came near, and spake unto him, and said, My father, if the prophet had bid thee do some great thing, wouldest thou not have done it? how much rather then, when he saith to thee, Wash, and be clean?

Then went he down, and dipped himself seven times in Jordan, according to the saying of the man of God: and his flesh came again like unto the flesh of a little child, and he was clean.

And he returned to the man of God, he and all his company, and came, and stood before him: and he said, Behold, now I know that there is no God in all the earth, but in Israel: now therefore, I pray thee, take a blessing of thy servant.

But he said, As the LORD liveth, before whom I stand, I will receive none. And he urged him to take it; but he refused.

And Naaman said, Shall there not then, I pray thee, be given to thy servant two mules' burden of earth? for thy servant will henceforth offer neither burnt offering nor sacrifice unto other gods, but unto the LORD.

In this thing the LORD pardon thy servant, that when my master goeth into the house of Rimmon to worship there, and he leaneth on my hand, and I *bow myself in the house of Rimmon: when I bow down myself in the house of Rimmon, the LORD pardon thy servant in this thing.*

And he said unto him, Go in peace. So he departed from him a little way.

But Gehazi, the servant of Elisha the man of God, said, Behold, my master hath spared Naaman this Syrian, in not receiving at his hands that which he brought: but, as the LORD liveth, I will run after him, and take somewhat of him.

So Gehazi followed after Naaman. And when Naaman saw him running after him, he lighted down from the chariot to meet him, and said, Is all well?

And he said, All is well. My master hath sent me, saying, Behold, even now there be come to me from mount Ephraim two young men of the sons of the prophets: give them, I pray thee, a talent of silver, and two changes of garments.

And Naaman said, Be content, take two talents. And he urged him, and bound two talents of silver in two bags, with two changes of garments, and laid them upon two of his servants; and they bare them before him.

And when he came to the tower, he took them from their hand, and bestowed them in the house: and he let the men go, and they departed.

2 Kings 5:1-24 (KJV)

Gehazi on the other hand was led by what he saw; he could not take his eyes off the nice things which Naaman brought.

It is important to establish in your spirit the fact that

you cannot rise beyond the levels of your perception.

If you do not see yourself by the standard of how God describes you and what God says you are, you would rise to that level. Your sight influences your direction; it determines your walk.

Your sight determines which way you move.

Whenever light is pointed at a direction, consciously or unconsciously, our eyes move in the direction of the source of light. It is important to see light by reason of your inner sight.

Your sight determines the peace you have, if you focus on the natural and things are going wrong, worry takes over. Your imagination is messed up and you begin to see yourself in situations where you should not be. The man who focuses on a life that is glorious finds his life being transformed into that which is his focus.

> *But we all, with open face beholding as in a glass the glory of the Lord, are changed into the same image from glory to glory, even as by the Spirit of the Lord.*
> *2 Corinthians 3:18 (KJV)*

Abraham fulfilled the law of sight and entered the greatest realm of his blessing when God gave him one of the tests of his life.

> *And the LORD said unto Abram, after that Lot was separated from him, Lift up now thine eyes, and look from the place where thou art northward, and southward, and eastward, and westward:*
> *For all the land which thou seest, to thee will I give it, and to thy seed for ever.*
> *And I will make thy seed as the dust of the earth: so that if a man can number the dust of the earth, then shall thy seed also be numbered.*
> *Arise, walk through the land in the length of it and in the breadth of it; for I will give it unto thee.*
> *Genesis 13:14-17 (KJV)*

As he worshipped God inside his tent on the night his nephew left, Abraham was told to look as far as his eyes could see.

Certainly that could not mean natural eyes, because no matter how plain and clear the topography was, at a time when there were no planes to take one above, there is a limit to what Abraham could have seen. By the eye of the Spirit Abraham saw the length and breadth of Palestine. God said as far as his eyes could see it would be given to him. If he had seen all of Europe and the United States, as far as Africa and Australia, it would have all been given to his sons. So Abraham was given the passport to possess what he saw.

The same God is rich unto all men. Let Him birth a new vision in your spirit and begin to believe what you see with the eye of your spirit and not what the enemy wants you to believe which is registered in the natural.

HOW TO BREAK THE SIGHT BARRIER?

1.   DEVELOP EAGLE SIGHT

Doth the eagle mount up at thy command, and make her nest on high?
She dwelleth and abideth on the rock, upon the crag of the rock, and the
strong place.
From thence she seeketh the prey, and her eyes behold afar off.
Job 39:27-29 (KJV)

One of the creatures of God we are compared to in the Bible is the eagle. It is one creature which far outshines most others. We are told in the book of Job that it sees its prey afar off, having a vision that is able to look two hundred and seventy five degrees. That enables the eagle to see almost from the front to the rear. One of the parts of the eagle that is fully developed from birth is its eyes. While it waits for the other parts to be developed, it can already see things from afar off.

Eagles can clearly identify things from close to a mile and pick objects the size of a ten pence coin from ten thousand feet. It has pectin inside its eyes which helps the eagle to navigate with extreme accuracy, so that even though it flies at thirty-five thousand feet above sea level it never misses its way, depending on its accurate sight for direction. The eagle also has a habit of picking a prey by reason of its sight, locking its vision and inner sight to the one object, and following through without deviation, even if it saw other things that could have been nicer.

The eagle focuses on what it had locked its eye on, in spite of the annoyance and distraction of other birds. Does that seem like the message for you? It effectively means that breakthrough or breakdown in life is often influenced by our ability to receive a vision from God and stay on it until the vision speaks. God in His omniscience used the eagle to compare with man.

Another incredible feature of the eagle's eye is a part of it called the fovea. The fovea gives the eagle extra accurate vision. The eagle has two foveas, this means that one fovea can work independently of the other. One of the fovea's contains the sharpest vision to look at things as they are moving ahead, while the other fovea can be receiving vision from another side.

Balance in breaking the sight barrier means that while you receive with the eye of the spirit you do not neglect the natural. The believer should be able to put both to action, so that with the natural eye he sees and makes judgement, but with the spiritual eye he receives direction from God. If your vision is not clear, your mind will become unstable.

A double minded man is unstable in all his ways.
James 1:8 (KJV)

The word double-minded here is from the Greek *dipsuchos* which means *two souls*. A man who is unstable and double-minded acts like he is of a split personality. To be led of God and to put your vision to practice you have got to learn to stay focused. You need to recognise the importance of what you see even with the natural eye, because your brain receives the images which your eye sees, and it tends to believe what you choose to focus on. Your brain in turn sends electro-messages through your body and your body reacts to what your brain has sent out.

2.   ACQUIRE SPIRITUAL SIGHT

It is important to look at life from the viewpoint of what God in Christ Jesus has done for you.

When your faith and confidence in Christ shapes your vision, you will see differently.

That the God of our Lord Jesus Christ, the Father of glory, may give unto you the spirit of wisdom and revelation in the knowledge of him:
The eyes of your understanding being enlightened; that ye may know what is the hope of his calling, and what the riches of the glory of his inheritance in the saints,
Ephesians 1:17-18 (KJV)

The church of Ephesus was one local church in all of Paul's writing whom he wrote, who had no doctrinal error to correct or ethical problems to address, but rather challenged them and gave them deep spiritual insight. One of the areas was the ability to allow the eye of their understanding to be enlightened so that they looked at life by insight.

.... and that the eyes of your heart may be flooded with light
Ephesians 1:18 (Mon)

that you may receive that inner illumination of the spirit
Ephesians 1:18 (Phillips)

Seeing things from a spiritual point of view means developing the ability to see your value, now that you are in Christ Jesus. Such a world view will determine how you see others. People who are quick to condemn others also have beams they need to remove from their eyes.

Developing spiritual insight would mean breaking the barriers which the seeds of wrong information that contradicts your vision have caused.

A spiritual perspective helps you to keep bringing up the picture of previous victory in the face of the present battle.

David said moreover, The LORD that delivered me out of the paw of the
lion, and out of the paw of the bear, he will deliver me out of the hand of
this Philistine. And Saul said unto David, Go, and the LORD be with thee.
1 Samuel 17:37 (KJV)

3.   USE YOUR IMAGINATION

The Webster's Comprehensive Dictionary of the English Language defines imagination as "the constructive or creative faculty, expressed in terms of images which either reproduce past experiences or combine them in ideal or creative forms." The church has tended to belittle or oppose the use of the imagination in the pursuit of their goals and visions for life, purely because people in the New Age movement do.

It would be unfortunate to take such a stand, because in effect a creative ability implanted in man would be going to waste. When God told the children of Israel that He was taking them to 'a land that was flowing with milk and honey, a land of green rolling hills', He certainly was painting a picture of a desired end, so that their faith was in tact in the face of challenges, since they could imagine a place so opposite to Egypt in topography and beauty.

Your imagination will help you to discover that inner ability to form mental pictures which do not exist materially, and as long as they agree with what God has ministered to you as His will for your life, you begin to prayerfully pursue. With the imagination people can create the negative or positive, they can imagine atmospheres of war or joyful situations. They can create images that cause them to worry or release happiness.

As long as the believer is of the understanding that only the counsel of the Lord will stand, it is not wrong for him to use the imagination, so long as he submits it to the Holy Spirit and says "What I see in my spirit, I desire and pray that one day it will come to pass".

Even opposers of imagination will certainly have had mental pictures of the person they would marry, the home they would live in, we call it 'the person of our dreams', 'the home of our dreams'. So we all use the imagination, it all depends on the name we call it. It is a great gift God has planted in you, use it, do not lose it! As you begin to see it in your spirit, and begin to walk in the counsel and will of God, you will have a mental picture of a desired end.

Think about why He said He would even do more than what we can imagine.

Now unto Him Who, by (in consequence of) the [action of His] power that is at work within us, is able to [carry out His purpose and] do superabundantly, far over and above all that we [dare] ask or think [infinitely beyond our highest prayers, desires, thoughts, hopes, or dreams]. Ephesians 3:20 (Amplified)

4.   USE YOUR HINDSIGHT

David said moreover, The LORD that delivered me out of the paw of the lion, and out of the paw of the bear, he will deliver me out of the hand of this Philistine. And Saul said unto David, Go, and the LORD be with thee. 1 Samuel 17:37 (KJV)

This is defined as insight into the nature and difficulty of a situation after the event or after the difficulties have been resolved. It is also called the rear sight. We are given the Old Testament in order to see examples in the old of the blessings we desire in the new.

Now all these things happened unto them for ensamples: and they are written for our admonition, upon whom the ends of the world are come. 1 Corinthians 10:11 (KJV)

The barrier the present problem wants to set for you will be shattered as you take the time to meditate on the goodness of God. Those who cannot think cannot thank, but if you can think of the days when God brought you out, when He opened a door where they said there was none, when He silenced the enemy. Remember how by a supernatural intervention He provided where there seemed to be no way of provision, every barrier in the present begins to be weakened and shattered.

5.   INSIGHT

Insight is the perception of the inner nature of a thing;

insight is necessary so that when you really understand the nature of a thing, it does not, hold you from overcoming it, because you have cracked its root especially if it is a problem.

Other synonyms of insight could be perception, cleverness, discernment, keenness, sharpness of mind, shrewdness, and sagacity.

6.   FORESIGHT

This is the act or capacity of foreseeing or looking forward.

It is the thoughtful care for the future; being able to anticipate the future before the future comes. A focus on the immediate and temporal makes many people not to look into the future and plan for the future. Foresight is your gift for winning while the enemy still sleeps.

Those who answer tomorrow's questions today will be in front when others are just waking up.

7. FAR SIGHT

Earlier on we saw how the eagle by an incredible far sight is able to differentiate objects from as far as a mile, and how it locks into the image of what it desires, and therefore moves with that image, thus keeping its prey within its reach.

Far sight is necessary in order to make provisions for years to come, in order to distil a vision that would chart the course of ones life.

By far sight one can focus on positive scenarios that help your faith, confidence and sense of purpose to rise because of the future you see. By far sight ideas, thoughts, concepts or visions can be registered on the tablet of the mind, and with prayer, a study of the Word and a continuous pursuit, it becomes a matter within reach.

The absence of hindsight, insight, foresight and far sight can create barriers to the next level of blessing which God is taking you to.

THE TOOLS FOR BREAKING BARRIERS

1.   DREAMS

The Webster's dictionary gives three definitions for the word dream which we want to look at:

1. A train of thoughts or images passing through the mind in sleep

2. A mental condition similar to that of one sleeping; abstractive imagining; daydreaming

3. A visionary idea, anticipation or fancy - also anything real having a dream-like quality

It is to the third definition that we look to for the steps to breaking the sight barriers

Dreams as it applies to envisioning, planning and seeing the future ahead is necessary.

A man without dreams is like a bird without wings, he cannot fly. You only make progress by the dreams you have in your heart. A man without a dream is at a dead end; he is short of ideas and cannot move on with life.

Dreams are essentially finding God's strength to do what God wants you to do and possess what He wants you to possess.

It is what equips you to fulfil your purpose on earth. Your dreams make everything you experience along the journey to become the tool for fulfilling your life.

And we know that all things work together for good to them that love God, to them who are the called according to his purpose.
Romans 8:28 (KJV)

2.   PERCEIVE

The word perception in the Hebrew is '*yada*'. It carries various meanings:

TO KNOW PROPERLY, ASCERTAIN BY SEEING, OBSERVE, CARE, RECOGNISE, ACKNOWLEDGE, ACQUAINT, AWARE, COMPREHEND, TO DISCOVER, MAKE TO KNOW, OR COME TO A PLACE OF KNOWING.

In the Greek it comes from the word '*theoreo*'. It carries the meaning:

DISCERN, BEHOLD, CONSIDER OR LOOK AT.

Perception means to see and understand beyond the surface meaning of a thing.

And he saith unto them, Are ye so without understanding also? Do ye not perceive, that whatsoever thing from without entereth into the man, it cannot defile him;
Mark 7:18 (KJV)

64

You may look at a thing but not perceive its meaning; i.e. you may not come to a place of understanding if God does not allow you.

> *And in them is fulfilled the prophecy of Esaias, which saith, By hearing ye shall hear, and shall not understand; and seeing ye shall see, and shall not perceive:*
> *Matthew 13:14 (KJV)*

Many people complain of reading the Bible and failing to understand it. Though they are not born again, they do not realise that you can look at the words and read, but the power to perceive is given to the people who are born of God and have His seed (nature) in them. Moses addressed the children of Israel when God renewed His covenant with them in Moab, and in the process, revealed the truth that the power of perception is only given by God.

> *Yet the LORD hath not given you an heart to perceive, and eyes to see, and ears to hear, unto this day.*
> *Deuteronomy 29:4 (KJV)*

People are afraid to use the word perception because of the teachings of cults and New Agers on ESP (Extra Sensory Perception). It always amazes me that the Church in its attempt to avoid being labelled as New Age, or being labelled erroneous, ends up throwing away truths that are fundamentally taught in Scripture.

If you want to keep your God-given vision alive, if the dreams and desires that He has put in your heart must come to pass, we must know how to perceive them, even when we do not see the physical manifestation.

The English philosopher William Blake said:

"Man's desires are limited by his perceptions, no-one can desire what he has not perceived."

Blake's observation simply confirms Scripture. It takes the eye of faith to see the end result before it comes. It takes the eye of faith to see what has already been done even when the situation looks contrary.

While we look not at the things which are seen, but at the things which are not seen: for the things which are seen are temporal; but the things which are not seen are eternal.
2 Corinthians 4:18 (KJV)

God created us in His image and He perceives things and calls them according to His perception.

That is why the scripture says in Hebrews 11:3

Through faith we understand that the worlds were framed by the word of God, so that things which are seen were not made of things which do appear.
Hebrews 11:3 (KJV)

God's perception is demonstrated in calling forth a perfectly ordered universe which should have taken millions of years to create, but which He created in six days.

His perception is revealed when:

He looked at a shepherd boy - David and He saw a king. That is perception.

He looked at a murderer - Moses and He saw a deliverer. That is perception.

He looked at a slave called Daniel and He saw a leader. That is perception.

He looked at Abram whose name meant 'father' and at ninety-nine was still childless and called him Abraham which means 'The Father of Nations'. God was not looking at Abraham's present state; He was looking at Abraham's future. That is perception.

God looks at brokenness, He sees healing.

This God whom we have described created you and put infinite value on you. In fact Jesus said you are more valuable than the whole of planet earth. After all "What shall it profit a man if he gains the whole world and loses his own soul?" (Mark 8:36) The real estate value of planet earth is nothing compared to one human being, but what you see is what you will become.

As I sit down writing, my mind recalls pictures of men and women I have known who in my simple judgement have twisted perceptions of who they are.

HOW DO I KNOW?

A twisted perception makes you want to be somebody else, therefore leading you to be envious and jealous.

A twisted perception makes people think the fulfilment of a dream and vision comes with their acquiring material things.

How do I know?

They end up worshipping the things which are meant to serve them. You can have material things. You may get a good job and still have a twisted perception, pursue the wrong dream and miss the mark.

Dreaming of course does not mean daydreaming; it is seeing yourself well, though sick. It is learning to speak the blessing of God, even when you are going through a shortage of supply. It is confessing the scripture that says you are an overcomer when you seem to be facing imminent defeat.

Ye are of God, little children, and have overcome them: because greater is he that is in you, than he that is in the world.
1 John 4:4 (KJV)

It is the ability to see the kingdom of God at work in you, when other grounds seem to be sinking sand. It is the ability to see yourself doing and achieving what was said to be impossible for you. Dreaming is that ability to see yourself come out of the rut into the right. Out of the gutter into glory, out of the prison into the palace, out of hell into heaven.

You must be ready though for those who would hate your dream, and those who would make your dream; you need both to break the barriers.

DREAM HATERS

Every dreamer and interpreter of dreams attracts dream haters. There is a lot of similarity between Joseph and Daniel. Both were sold to slavery, interpreted dreams of kings, had dreams, and became Prime Ministers. They also shared a similarity of having dream haters. The moment Joseph announced his dreams and visions he provoked the envy and hatred of his brothers.

And Joseph dreamed a dream, and he told it his brethren: and they hated him yet the more.

And his brethren envied him; but his father observed the saying.
Genesis 37:5, 11 (KJV)

Whenever you announce your vision of evangelism, building the Kingdom of God, reaching more souls for Jesus, and ministering to the sick, demonic dream haters will be put into action by the enemy.

HIS BROTHERS envied him. This brings out the truth that two or three years after a person is born again his circle of social contacts are essentially believers. If he suffers and is hurt it is not likely to be from unbelievers.

The second major dream hater he encountered was POTIPHAR'S WIFE. We have referred to her in a previous chapter, but her action brings to remembrance Proverbs 6:26:

69

For by means of a whorish woman a man is brought to a piece of bread: and
the adultress will hunt for the precious life.
Proverbs 6:26 (KJV)

Following his experience in the house of Potiphar, he now finds himself in prison. Potiphar forgot all the young man's previous good deeds. We do not know if he put Joseph in the king's prison because he did not believe his wife. In the sight of men all the good deeds we may have done are wiped away in one day by one mistake, or evil false report which may have no proof or foundation.

Yet did not the chief butler remember Joseph, but forgat him.
Genesis 40:23 (KJV)

When we put our confidence in man, close friends, associates or relations they may disappoint us. Throughout the Bible we are only instructed to love man and trust God. There is not a place in scripture where we are told to trust in man.

One of the dream haters that could destroy a person's future is putting his confidence in the wrong place.

DREAM TAKERS

Dream takers basically are states of our own emotional experiences which we may have had, which can freeze the dreams and aspirations God has put in our hearts to achieve. I have listed the following: complacency, fear, tradition, mediocrity, short term thinking, fatigue and doubt etc. If dreams are God's original intention for our lives, if they are the compass

70

to guide us from wasting our time on this planet, then we will do everything to acquire the vision and dream God has for us.

Let us look at these dream takers one by one. As you read, if you are held in the trap of any of them, make a quality decision and shake it off in the Name of the Lord.

1. COMPLACENCY

'It does not matter what we do, God will bless our efforts.' This kind of statement is a prognosis of ministries, ministers, and lives of believers who want to settle for the enemy called 'average'. You cannot be an average Christian and receive a full time reward. God cares what we do with our time and how we live our lives here.

If He does not care, He would not have given you the vision and dreams that had crossed your heart at one time or the other, which you probably refused to pursue because you were unsure if they were from Him.

2. FEAR

The simplest way to define fear is:

False
Evidence
Appearing
Real

Can you imagine what could have happened if Joseph's dream had been frustrated by a haranguing fear instilled by his father, brothers, Potiphar experience, or his own presumption?

Many do not dream any new dream because the previous dreams they had never materialised, or when they shared it with someone their sixteen-foot dream was reduced to six feet.

There are people who are afraid of failure and people who are afraid of succeeding because they know success attracts criticism.

3. TRADITION

This is the way I have always done it and it has always worked for me. Why do I need to change?

Tradition is a very strong blockade to dreaming a new dream. It is a clog in the wheel to fulfilling God's visions and dreams for us.

4. MEDIOCRITY

Mediocrity is a dream taker and probably one of the worst.

If you are mediocre you will be busy or engaged in fruitless programmes and not achieving your full potential. Mediocre people like to be seen to be busy. Busyness does not mean achievement. Many do not quantify what they are doing, to see how valuable it is to the fulfilling of their dreams and visions. If you have a plumber in a company, who takes two hours to fix a broken pipe, he is not mediocre, but if in the attempt to save forty pounds, the Executive Director of the same company spends four hours of company time doing the same job, he would have wasted more money and quality time in a job he is unskilled to do as a highly paid executive.

5. SHORT-TERM THINKING

God's vision for your life is long-term and is intended to outlive your short-term thinking, as goals for your life extend into eternity. Consequently when Joseph was about to die at one hundred and thirty years, he made the children of Israel swear that his bones would be buried in Canaan.

In the book of Hebrews, Chapter 11, where the roll call of those who lived by faith is stated, the outstanding thing recorded about Joseph was his instructions concerning his bones.

By faith Joseph, when he died, made mention of the departing of the children of Israel; and gave commandment concerning his bones.
Hebrews 11:22 (KJV)

The question is - what is so special about bones? There is a lot.

Joseph foresaw the slavery, he saw the children of Israel give up God's long-time vision of settling in Canaan.

He therefore gave instructions that his vision must outlive him. The children of Israel must go back to Canaan. All through slavery in Egypt, for four hundred and thirty years, Joseph's instruction was one source of their motivation. It is almost like they were saying to each other, 'we must go back, we must carry Joseph's bones, there is still a place to reach, there is another land, there is a future.'

In your divine destiny God has put enough in you to continue after your death. You are a blessing to you generation and the one to come.

6. FATIGUE

There is a point when tiredness comes in and we lose a clear definition of our vision and our thrust. We lose the spiritual and mental agility for running with our God-given vision. Fatigue will try to twist your vision. The best thing to do at such a time is to wait on the Lord for a renewal of strength.

> *But they that wait upon the LORD shall renew their strength; they shall mount up with wings as eagles; they shall run, and not be weary; and they shall walk, and not faint.*
> *Isaiah 40:31 (KJV)*

7. DOUBT

> *"And to whom swear he that they should not enter into his rest, but to them that believed not? So we see that they could not enter in because of unbelief."*
> *Hebrews 3:18-19 (KJV)*

Doubt is the greatest thief of God's blessings.

The things God will manifest to your renewed heart will be more than you can perceive, but once you are able to perceive, you need to believe. When you believe, you will be able to conceive them and achieve them. If you doubt, you limit God, because God has committed Himself to honour whatever is accompanied by faith.

8. STAGNATION

Stagnation may be the result if we do not remain in motion with our God-given idea.

Many people get riveted to what they consider success now. Being hooked to the glory of yesterday's success could be a major deterrent to the greater potential we have. When people stagnate they join the mass majority who never achieve their God-given vision. As a matter of fact most people operate only on ten percent of their God-given ability.

9. PROCRASTINATION

'Procrastination' they say, is the thief of all time.

The uncertainty of the future and the success we know from the past easily deceives and makes people procrastinate on the steps which would have brought the fulfilment of God's vision for their life.

The physical blessing and progress of Lot in the city of Sodom made him hesitate when the angels of the Lord came to take him out of imminent danger.

"And while he lingered, the men laid hold upon his hand, and upon the hand of his wife, and upon the hand of his two daughters; the LORD being merciful unto him: and they brought him forth, and set him without the city."
Genesis 19:16 (KJV)

Procrastination could also be a product of the uncertainties of the future but:

- if hunger is proof that food exists
- if thirst is proof that liquid or water exists

THE DEATH OF DREAMS

Let us quickly look at these negative things which are likely to happen to a woman who conceives and is about to give birth to a child. We have earlier shown the importance of conception, the vision, and ideas God gives us until its fulfilment. Many visions, ideas, and God-given dreams have ended the following ways.

1. Abortion: When a God-given dream, vision or idea is suddenly quashed because of setbacks, and the inability to fulfil it.

2. Stillborn: It is a great emotional and spiritual trauma if a person perceives an idea, carries it through a time of spiritual conception and prayer, but it resulted in a vision which is 'dead on arrival' when the time of the delivery of the idea came.

3. Premature Birth: It is important not to procrastinate when God gives you a winning idea, but it is of a greater importance when we value spiritual timing with whatever vision or goal we want to carry out. Joseph did not force the fulfilment of his dream until the time was right. When God calls a man, sometimes he shows him a vision of large crusades, a large church, breakthroughs, etc.

This is because God is using what is called incentive motivation; that is using the positive to challenge a person. What many people do not realise is that the vision, large crusades, big congregations or other successes, may end up being the product of ten years of faithfulness and not of immediate labour.

4.Complication: Vision, dreams and the redemptive revelation of God have a powerful way of gripping the heart, making a visionary want to 'scale over a wall'. When complications come, some have surrendered their visions. They prepared for success but they did not see complications as part of the process of the fulfilment of their God-given dream.

5. Small Wombs: Many women may never have children because their womb is too small to carry a normal pregnancy. God cannot exceed the limits of your visions and dreams. He cannot make to happen what you do not see Him achieve in your life. What you do not see, you do not receive.

ACQUIRE AND PURSUE VISION

Where there is no vision, the people perish: but he that keepeth the law,
happy is he.
Proverbs 29:18 (KJV)

And the LORD answered me, and said, Write the vision, and make it plain
upon tables, that he may run that readeth it.
For the vision is yet for an appointed time, but at the end it shall speak,
and not lie: though it tarry, wait for it; because it will surely come,
it will not tarry.
Habakkuk 2:2-3 (KJV)

There are eight ways to make this happen. Do not neglect any of them or it will frustrate your pursuit:

1.   THE RIGHT VISION

The subject of vision is important in breaking down the sight barrier,

albeit it is now popular in the body of Christ for people to set their visions and goals, but because it is popular does not mean it is done properly. It is important for you to set out and achieve your purpose in life by pursuing what is the right vision for you.

The vision will be right if you are not caught in the trap of what is copy cat, lockstep and mediocrity.

In other words not repeating what others have done, but getting to know what God has in store for you which may exceed that of people you even hold in high esteem. Vision is what authenticates your life, it takes you from being a mere copy or synthetic living, to being the real thing, to being authentic.

The right vision will impart a picture of your desired goal, it would also clarify what your destiny really is.

The right vision will be one unique passion you have which you cannot shake off, shrug off or run away from. It may not seem great to others but it will be an all consuming desire.

George Mueller had a desire to build a home for orphans, Kenneth Hagin had a strong passion to teach faith, Oral Roberts had a passion to build a university, Benny Hinn is turned on by the sight that provokes him to minister to the sick. Your vision will be right if it triggers the desire to fulfil what God has planted in your heart.

It is the right vision if it is operating as your eye into the future, causing you to see beyond the natural and into the supernatural.

It is the right vision if it increases your hope and faith level so that with the things that seem daunting and unachievable, you come to an understanding that step by step everything is within reach.

The right vision would help you to locate your calling and begin to pursue it so that you are not fulfilling the call other people have for you, but what God inevitably had prepared for you.

2. WRITE THE VISION

Vision is the ability to anticipate, prepare and make provisions for the future; it is that which brings together hindsight, insight, foresight, far sight and imagination.

It uses them effectively to co-ordinate a desired goal and method for arrival. A man without vision would be a slave of other people's visions. Progress in life is made by the picture we see.

It must be clearly written so that it empowers the visionary to pursue a desired tomorrow. It is that which would help him to hope and dream and pray for the things which are yet to be within his reach.

Now faith is the substance of things hoped for, the evidence of things not seen.
Hebrews 11:1 (KJV)

You need to write your vision because it is your key to authentic living.

A man who has not written it enough for him to pursue it will become a mediocre and a copycat who is into a lockstep mentality. You end up following others and only making progress by using your friends to determine where you should be.

Vision is the unique calling of the believer to fulfil his life and it is that which helps him to achieve.

It is the eye he has to the future, that is why the enemy is working overtime to scuttle it. Vision that will keep you from living a bankrupt life; vision is what will make you grow in this kingdom, because God Himself is a visionary.

A man who cannot see beyond His nose has jeopardised the whole of his destiny and that of the generations that will come out of him. Vision is your basis for living because without sight there is no going.

The written vision is better summarised by the acrostic P.O.M.C.A. - Preview of My Coming Attraction. God instructed the prophet Habakkuk to write the vision and make it plain. What you keep at the back of your mind may never manifest before your eyes. So if the vision is that major, write it down because it will help you to paint a mental portrait of where you are going. It will help to determine your destiny, so that you are not carried off track by the immediate and the temporary.

You are as great or as small as the vision you define from your heart.

So when you write it down and make it plain, your life becomes a success and not a waste. Your vision helps you to locate your place in the programme of God; it helps you to innovate without waiting for problems. Many never act until there is a problem, that kind of lifestyle is what I call the fire brigade mentality - no action until there is a problem.

The importance of writing your vision cannot be over-emphasised because it is the vision you elevate and the idea you talk about which will become the reality of your life,

and what you build the whole of your destiny upon.

3.   READ THE VISION

It is not enough to have one's vision nicely written and tucked away in a diary. It is important to keep it before you and remind yourself of where you are going so that you become an achiever in the affairs of life.

Written visions that are from God are revelatory in nature, they expose to you the programme God has for you.

The knowledge vision brings informs your decision, if there is no vision, your decision is informed by people's opinion, the temporary and the needs around. People who run around looking for several counsellors to input into their life immediately mirror a life without a vision.

Vision helps you to fulfil the law of sight, the ability to see and possess what you have already understood in your heart.

If nothing is craved nothing is supplied. A vision clearly written and read regularly means you are on your way to achieve the purpose of God.

4.   RATE THE VISION

Your vision is not big enough until it shocks your peers.

A beggar sat on a bench in the park. Dirty, his dog too was just as he was. Not long after an artist came and started drawing an image of the beggar. He drew the beggar, and at the end he showed him. It was not exactly as the beggar thought it would be. He said "that could not be me". He drew the beggar in a nice, well-cleaned suit, his dog cleaned up and shining. The beggar was wearing the best of clothes money could ever buy, and said, "who is that?" The artist replied "that's the you I see in you". The beggar responded "if that's the me you see in me, I choose to be what you saw in me".

You need a vision that would increase your speed in life, not the one that is just playing catch up and trying to meet up with the Joneses.

You need the vision that would make you live beyond your natural ability, that will cause you to run and do things beyond you have done before. A vision that would rate in the sight of God is the one that can shape the destiny of your children's children and grandchildren. Rate your vision, because it will determine the distance you make in the race of life. Many run, only one obtains. Have the vision that will make you obtain what you were sent to this planet to achieve.

5. RUN WITH THE VISION

Know ye not that they which run in a race run all, but one receiveth the prize? So run, that ye may obtain.
And every man that striveth for the mastery is temperate in all things. Now they do it to obtain a corruptible crown; but we an incorruptible.
I therefore so run, not as uncertainly; so fight I, not as one that beateth the air:
But I keep under my body, and bring it into subjection: lest that by any means, when I have preached to others, I myself should be a castaway.
1 Corinthians 9:24-27 (KJV)

To write and rate your vision without running with it, is like having a good idea but doing nothing and hoping that it would just work. Nothing works until somebody makes it work. It is important that you run with your vision. It is yours and nobody else's. Nobody owes you any responsibility to make your vision happen. You need to turn your vision from potential to an active force by reason of your own activity.

Until the man by the beautiful gate stood up, his healing was not completed.

Until the man by the pool of Bethsaida picked his bed and walked, he could have stayed there beyond the thirty-eight years. Until the woman with the issue of blood took action, her haemorrhage did not cease. Walk out your vision, nothing works until you act on it. Dreams only come true when you wake up to make it happen.

86

If a man dreams of eating the best meal on earth, he needs to wake up and cook it. If you do not do something about your vision, all you will have is regrets. Be committed to your vision. People read your actions and follow as far as you lead them. Let your vision make your life unstoppable. Let it increase your speed in life. Let the mere thought of what it could be if you fulfil your destiny, cause you to run and not be weary.

6. ROOTED IN THE VISION

Every good thing will be opposed; your vision has enemies. Satan wants to frustrate your climb in life. You must understand that in spite of the pain, the problem or persecutions you face, your vision has possibilities and opportunities. Do not let what you are going through, stop where you are going to. Refuse to let temporary setbacks shift your focus, it is time to break the barriers and see your destiny.

Therefore, my beloved brethren, be ye stedfast, unmoveable, always abounding in the work of the Lord, forasmuch as ye know that your labour is not in vain in the Lord.
1 Corinthians 15:58 (KJV)

Do not let the enemy abort your vision.

If that happens you have already condemned your future. Stay focused, this will make you move further ahead of tomorrow than you are today. A broken focus is a reason for accidents. Be rooted in the vision as you get the vision straight and pursue it. Twisted vision makes you want to be somebody else. When you are not rooted in what God says you are and what God wants you to be, you will not walk in jealousy and become envious of what other people are.

You need to be rooted in the vision and calling of God for your life because your vision will focus your

life from panic and crisis, to success orientation.

This will help you and give you the ability to say no to what God has not led you to. It is time to resign from the company of those who move from one career to the other; from one place to the other; from one spouse to the other. Do things by vision and your life will be stable and fulfilling.

7.   REACH THE VISION

The beginner is not the worker; the scripture says the person who endures to the end is the one who will be saved.

There are many beginners, but few finishers, be one of them. The world does not crown those who did not finish and if you must finish, it is important to finish well.

It is important to reach your vision and complete it, because it does not take a lot of people in your life to bring out your destiny.

All you need is to have the right people around you.

You need to reach your vision because the future which you are pursuing will only respond to you if you are ready to go all the way. How many people have launched good things but did not have the strength, boldness and grace to complete it?

Reach your vision, it is a tragedy when visions are aborted or prematurely born.

It is even worse if it results in being stillborn. Reach your vision my friend, you are responsible for finding and following what God has destined you to become. It is time to stop blaming your father for being poor, your mother for not being rich and your teacher for frustrating you in maths class. It is time to know that with God you are now more than a majority. Reach your vision, your future and function depends on it.

Reach your vision, there is no future in jobs or certificates. It is not in the new career or the name or a new kind of innovation. It is not in lotteries or gambling. It is in vision. How may I you may ask?. Start with what you see and hear, and that is why we are breaking those barriers. What you hear affects what you see and what you see becomes what you get.

Break those barriers that say you cannot receive certain blessings.

Because you were born on the wrong side of the city does not mean you will die there. Make up your mind and endeavour to break free from comfort zones. It is so easy to look for warm places like reptiles do and hide oneself and wait for easy food, and easy breakthroughs. It is important to reach out and break free from every comfort zone.

Appoint mentors to your life, people who would help you to be signposts on the road to success.

Those who will point you to the right direction do not have to like you, you just need them to help you to be whom God wants you to be.

Put your life's goal in one clear concise statement and commit yourself to it. If you do not, you would be a wandering generality.

Stay away from those who hate your dreams and make no investment in your life and yet make a demand on it.

It is important if you must reach where you are going you cannot surround yourself with VNP's - Very Needing People and VDP's - Very Draining People. Look for and surround yourself with vision builders, vision makers, mentors, healthy friends, loved ones and families who sow good seed into your life, who fill your emotional cup. You cannot make it alone, you need them to reach where you are going.

8.   RESULTS OF VISION

We have clearly established that vision is a number one breaker of the barrier of sight. In other words whatever wants to limit your sight must change when you get a vision.

Let me share some of the blessings that will begin to come your way by reason of vision. Through vision you can access the provisions God has for you and not settle for the leftovers the enemy says you deserve. By vision you are able to make quality, godly and clear decisions that would lift your level of performance and playing field.

By reason of vision you will come into a realm of productivity beyond you have ever done.

By reason of vision Abraham moved from a man who was left alone by his nephew to being rich in cattle. The possession of vision is the end of all struggles. Struggle ends where vision takes over.

When you allow your vision as God has given you, to begin to shape your decision and pursuit in life, stress departs; the peace of God that passes understanding fills your life.

And the peace of God, which passeth all understanding, shall keep your hearts and minds through Christ Jesus.
Philippians 4:7 (KJV)

The presence of vision takes your life from a reader of history, to become a maker of history.

When vision is in your heart it fires you up to solve problems, not to gather problems. You do not run around seeking who may counsel you; you become enthroned in the blessing of God and an answer to many people's questions. The presence of vision increases your confidence in God, as you see Him make the vision come to pass.

Vision is your reason for being able to travel straight in a clear direction when others are confused as to which way to turn at the crossroads of life.

Vision takes your life from explanation to exclamation! You become a testimony to your friends and foes.

When vision informs every decision of your life, new habits are formed and a new atmosphere is developed around you.

By reason of the vision that is from above you are able to focus on the invisible God who can do incredible things that were said to be impossible. Let your vision speak and blessing will be loaded in your future.

Allow your vision to speak, and success will be the manifestation people see in your future.

Vision makes your life authentic, not synthetic, fulfilled not full of fear. You will not die even in your winter; your vision will remind you that spring is around the corner.

Do not let those who steal visions, kill dreams and abort goals, negotiate you out of what God is speaking in your heart.

Focus on the promises of God and the vision He has shown you for life. In your weak moments, keep the vision alive. Keep bringing up the picture of your victory on the screen of your mind. Let the vision of victory you see shape your future, reject and refuse every attempt of worry to steal your joy. Make yourself focus on what God has already said. May your eyes be blessed to see great things.

And he turned him unto his disciples, and said privately, Blessed are the eyes which see the things that ye see:
Luke 10:23 (KJV)

KEEP AN UNBROKEN FOCUS

This far we have established the fact that God has done everything to help the believer break every sight barrier and turn his sight to a doorway, into a life of bliss, blessing and favour. God constantly painted a picture of the positive for the children of Israel to see that the plans He had for them were always good and not evil.

For I know the thoughts that I think toward you, saith the LORD, thoughts of peace, and not of evil, to give you an expected end.
Jeremiah 29:11 (KJV)

He allowed them to see the miracles which He performed in the wilderness. They saw the cloud of glory follow them by day and it became a pillar of fire by night. He painted a picture of a land of fruitfulness which they were going to possess. The scriptures describe the luscious greenness of the mountains of Israel before they stepped on the grounds.

The imagination of this people which was used by God was to give them a picture of a life far more satisfying than the dryness of Egypt they knew before. God described the land they were going to as a land which could not be compared to the hardships they had experienced.

It fired a desire in them:
1. For freedom
2. For something of their own
3. For a place better than they had ever been.

For the believer today who must like the children of Israel enjoy what God has in store, it is important to maintain an unbroken focus. It is the person you see and the picture you expect that determines what you receive.

Who seeing Peter and John about to go into the temple asked an alms.
And Peter, fastening his eyes upon him with John, said, Look on us.
And he gave heed unto them, expecting to receive something of them.
Then Peter said, Silver and gold have I none; but such as I have give I thee:
In the name of Jesus Christ of Nazareth rise up and walk.
Acts 3:3-6 (KJV)

The importance of focus cannot be over emphasised in your Christian life. It is so crucial that you could not look elsewhere, but where your answer will come from.

Wherefore seeing we also are compassed about with so great a cloud of witnesses, let us lay aside every weight, and the sin which doth so easily beset us, and let us run with patience the race that is set before us,
Hebrews 12:1 (KJV)

Its absence could cause a failure or a fall, even in the most mundane places in your life. The absence of focus can make you walk into a trap which could have been avoidable, but because you were distracted the absence of focus could cost you and cause you to bump into the things that should not have been in your way in the first place. Its absence may mean that you are saying the things you should not say, and are busy doing the things you should not do.

Unfocused people also go to places they should not go, and when there is no focus they are busy in other people's matters. Focus is so important if you must take your eye off evil and keep it on that which is God glorifying.

97

The LORD hath taken away thy judgments, he hath cast out thine enemy:
the king of Israel, even the LORD, is in the midst of thee: thou shalt not see
evil any more.
Zephaniah 3:15 (KJV)

If you must break the barrier of sight which has been with you from childhood and use your sight as a doorway to blessing, you must be focused.

Your sight is necessary for you to succeed in every facet of your Christian life. If insight, revelation and light will be available, it will be dependent on how focused you are and matter-of-fact the level of your focus determines the strength of light available to you.

The light of the body is the eye: therefore when thine eye is single, thy whole
body also is full of light; but when thine eye is evil, thy body also is full of
darkness.
Luke 11:34 (KJV)

We have already established the importance of breaking the barrier of sight and that is in a nutshell the fact that you will not possess what you cannot see. You would only receive what you see with your mind's eye or the eye of the spirit. In fact your prayer is better focused when your spirit sees the desired end before you started praying, and until you focus enough to see it, you cannot function enough to manifest it.

The degree of a man's focus is revealed in the kind of wisdom which flows from him.

He cutteth out rivers among the rocks; and his eye seeth every precious thing.
Job 28:10 (KJV)

It helps him to know that before blessing can come into his hand, it must first come through his inner sight.

Say not ye, There are yet four months, and then cometh harvest? behold, I say unto you, Lift up your eyes, and look on the fields; for they are white already to harvest.
John 4:35 (KJV)

If you see the harvest when others are saying it is not harvest time, then you are operating in the field of focus.

THE TRANSFORMATION OF LIFE COMES BY REASON OF FOCUS.

If a man begins to concentrate on a thing he becomes that thing. What you focus on is what you are likely to be changed into. If you focus on a life of purity and holiness, you become that. When you focus your life, transformation follows in that area.

Whether blessing is received or failure is experienced in any sphere of life would also be determined by how focused one is.

When Peter and John accosted the man by the Beautiful Gate who was brought there paralysed, their focus was the revealed will of God. It determined their ability to be a blessing to a man that had hitherto been given up by his family.

> *And Peter, fastening his eyes upon him with John, said, Look on us.*
> *Acts 3:4 (KJV)*

Beloved, it is time for you to fasten your eyes on the things God wants to do, and you will not fail. If you keep looking at what the enemy is doing you would not receive what God has planned for you. But when you look to God light would shine and where you had known shame, you will see blessing.

> *They looked unto him, and were lightened: and their faces were not*
> *ashamed.*
> *Psalm 34:5 (KJV)*

FOCUSED PEOPLE DEMONSTRATE THE POWER OF GOD

They are able to bring healing to those who are broken.

> *And there sat a certain man at Lystra, impotent in his feet, being a cripple*
> *from his mother's womb, who never had walked:*
> *The same heard Paul speak: who stedfastly beholding him, and perceiving*
> *that he had faith to be healed,*
> *Said with a loud voice, Stand upright on thy feet. And he leaped and walked.*
> *Acts 14:8-10 (KJV)*

The man in this passage focused steadfastly on Paul perceiving that he would receive something, he was not disappointed. What you concentrate on will either deliver or destroy you.

If you must minister to other people focus is also necessary because

nobody can minister beyond what he sees in the spirit realm.

The vision you see will determine the dimension of your operation. It is possible to be surrounded by demon entities and even think it is of the Lord.

Paul by discernment knew the spirit that operated in the young lady in Philippi.

FOCUSING IS LIKE ENVISIONING

The sight you see in the spirit realm determines the blessing you receive in the earth realm.

While we look not at the things which are seen, but at the things which are not seen: for the things which are seen are temporal; but the things which are not seen are eternal.
2 Corinthians 4:18 (KJV)

So if you cannot shop with your eyes closed do not attempt to receive in the spirit realm without focus.

When you see it in the realm of the spirit you can call it forth into the earthly realm. It is the ability to see those things before their manifestation, that makes a man of faith to call the things that be not as though they were.

(As it is written, I have made thee a father of many nations,) before him whom he believed, even God, who quickeneth the dead, and calleth those things which be not as though they were.
Romans 4:17 (KJV)

So my friend it is time for you to receive what God has for you.

WHY MUST YOU FOCUS?

It is important to use your power of focus in breaking the sight barrier,

because what you focus on determines what you master.

What you focus on determines the amount of anointing that also rests upon your life. If you concentrate on Christ you become filled with Him.

Wherefore seeing we also are compassed about with so great a cloud of witnesses, let us lay aside every weight, and the sin which doth so easily beset us, and let us run with patience the race that is set before us, Looking unto Jesus the author and finisher of our faith; who for the joy that was set before him endured the cross, despising the shame, and is set down at the right hand of the throne of God.
Hebrews 12:1-2 (KJV)

The chief reason for insecurity, failure and broken lives is really a broken focus.

When people have nothing positive to focus on, all roads will lead where they think they are going.

A double minded man is unstable in all his ways.
James 1:8 (KJV)

Every aspect of the Christian life also needs to be focused for it to maximise results.

Your prayer needs to be focused in order to receive specific answers.

> *But let him ask in faith, nothing wavering. For he that wavereth is like a*
> *wave of the sea driven with the wind and tossed.*
> *For let not that man think that he shall receive any thing of the Lord.*
> *James 1:6-7 (KJV)*

You need to focus on the Word of God not the circumstance around you in order to be a winner in the affairs of life.

The focus on the Word is what makes you a victor and a winner.

> *There shall no man be able to stand before you: for the LORD your God*
> *shall lay the fear of you and the dread of you upon all the land that ye shall*
> *tread upon, as he hath said unto you.*
> *Deuteronomy 11:25 (KJV)*

The race you are running, the journey you have already started can only be completed in total success if it is informed by focus.

Therefore shall ye lay up these my words in your heart and in your soul, and bind them for a sign upon your hand, that they may be as frontlets between your eyes.

And ye shall teach them your children, speaking of them when thou sittest in thine house, and when thou walkest by the way, when thou liest down, and when thou risest up.

And thou shalt write them upon the door posts of thine house, and upon thy gates:

Deuteronomy 11:18-20 (KJV)

WHAT TO FOCUS ON

Someone said "Do not focus on the greatness of your problem, but the greatness of the promises of God". Let us start with focusing on the purpose of God for your life.

Not as though I had already attained, either were already perfect: but I follow after, if that I may apprehend that for which also I am apprehended of Christ Jesus.
Brethren, I count not myself to have apprehended: but this one thing I do, forgetting those things which are behind, and reaching forth unto those things which are before,
I press toward the mark for the prize of the high calling of God in Christ Jesus.
Philippians 3:12-14 (KJV)

Purpose is the total summary of your assignment.

It is where you are going in life. A lack of focus would make you pursue other people's kind of life and miss what you are called to be and do. Focus also on the calling of God for your life, you have been called to an inheritance which cannot fade.

Focus on God's revealed plan for your life which He has spoken to you through your spirit man.

But as it is written, Eye hath not seen, nor ear heard, neither have entered into the heart of man, the things which God hath prepared for them that love him.
1 Corinthians 2:9 (KJV)

Focus on Jesus so that you would not be carried away by the roaring troubles around you.

And Peter answered him and said, Lord, if it be thou, bid me come unto thee on the water.
And he said, Come. And when Peter was come down out of the ship, he walked on the water, to go to Jesus.
But when he saw the wind boisterous, he was afraid; and beginning to sink, he cried, saying, Lord, save me.
Matthew 14:28-30 (KJV)

It is important to focus on Jesus so that you will not succumb to the roaring sea of troubles that want to distract you and become a barrier to what you are called to do.

Always remember in your journey that even temporary distractions are deadly. They are Satan's tools to stop you from permanent breakthroughs. You cannot afford them. Those who will make it in this Kingdom in these last days cannot afford to be distracted by the arm of flesh.

HOW TO STAY FOCUSED

The modern man is prone to more distractions than all generations that have ever lived. Particularly since he is surrounded by symbols of modernism and technological progress. He is surrounded by things which offer temporary solutions and satisfaction, but distract from eternal purposes.

A young man who is called of God today to minister may immediately be distracted by the various opportunities he could find. He could be distracted by those who are ready to pay almost anything for the skills he possesses. It is God's plan to bless the believer, but it is important to find that blessing in pursuing your ultimate purpose rather than seeking the blessing while being distracted from your purpose.

To focus on the reason for your existence, to keep your sight on your destination, you must primarily put God in the centre of all that you do.

If your eyes are on Him, evil will not steal your attention.

For he shall be as a tree planted by the waters, and that spreadeth out her roots by the river, and shall not see when heat cometh, but her leaf shall be green; and shall not be careful in the year of drought, neither shall cease from yielding fruit.
Jeremiah 17:8 (KJV)

Many people are languishing having fallen into the ditches and the valleys of life. Some of them are walking in the dry places of life because they have taken their eyes from where they should be focused. This is not your portion, and it must not be your experience. Ask the Lord to remove those blemishes which may hinder you from focusing on Him.

Then learn to pray, seek God's face so that every precious thing hidden hitherto from you will be exposed to you, so that you are not directed and distracted by the temporary and miss what is there for you.

It is of interest to realise that this our planet in which mankind has lived for thousands of years; all the precious things being discovered today that make life convenient for modern man, were always there not and imported from another planet. But what people focus on determines what they see. The cave-man focused on his temporary problems; he focused on the grounds but did not see the treasures inside the grounds.

Begin to declare that you will not miss all the great opportunities, the precious promises, the doors God is opening, the supernatural favours which are coming your way and the things which God is setting in motion.

And the LORD said unto Abram, after that Lot was separated from him, Lift up now thine eyes, and look from the place where thou art northward, and southward, and eastward, and westward:
Genesis 13:14 (KJV)

In John 4:35, Jesus said the harvest was ready to be picked. In the times of Jesus the people were going by the calendar, Jesus was going by inner focus. They thought it was not yet time, He saw it was time, the fields were all ready for harvesting. There is a field ready for harvest around you, do not take your cue from what people say. Listen to the voice of the Holy Spirit. Those who are led by Him, are the matured children of God.

For as many as are led by the Spirit of God, they are the sons of God.
Romans 8:14 (KJV)

Ask God for the ability to focus on His perfect will, so that you do not miss what He has in store for you. Life is too brief to spend it pursuing the things you have no business checking out. Understand that when Jesus said in that verse "Lift up your eyes", He was already declaring what may not be the right time in the natural but what was already set in motion in the supernatural realm.

"Lift up your eyes" in John 4:35 meant it is time to stop bowing to situations and start looking up to the One who answers prayer. Lift up your eyes and see God settling you down in His purpose. Stop bowing your head to the immediate challenges around you. Lift up your eyes and see healing, God's desire for you is not to perish on the bed of languishing. Begin to see the day of your restoration in front of you. Begin to see things that have never worked for you coming to pass.

Lift up your eyes and receive answers to your prayer.

Answers that have been put in place before the need arose. When the Word of God said lift up your eyes it is also instructing you to not look at anything else but what the Word promises. Making the Word of God and the purpose of God your primary focus.

David too had cause to be distracted but he quickly cried out that he would look only to the hills from whence comes his help.

> *I will lift up mine eyes unto the hills, from whence cometh my help.*
> *Psalms 121:1 (KJV)*

Jacob possibly knew the power of focus, when given the opportunity to take the fruits of the sheep that bore, he made the pregnant sheep to focus on the rods he had painted, and they became what he desired them to be. If it worked in that realm it cannot fail in your life.

> *And Jacob took him rods of green poplar, and of the hazel and chesnut tree; and pilled white strakes in them, and made the white appear which was in the rods.*
> *And he set the rods which he had pilled before the flocks in the gutters in the watering troughs when the flocks came to drink, that they should conceive when they came to drink.*
> *And the flocks conceived before the rods, and brought forth cattle ringstraked, speckled, and spotted.*
> *And Jacob did separate the lambs, and set the faces of the flocks toward the ringstraked, and all the brown in the flock of Laban; and he put his own flocks by themselves, and put them not unto Laban's cattle.*
> *And it came to pass, whensoever the stronger cattle did conceive, that Jacob laid the rods before the eyes of the cattle in the gutters, that they might conceive among the rods.*
> *But when the cattle were feeble, he put them not in: so the feebler were*

> *Laban's, and the stronger Jacob's.*
> *And the man increased exceedingly, and had much cattle, and maidservants,*
> *and menservants, and camels, and asses.*
> *Genesis 30:37-43 (KJV)*

To be without physical sight, one might be able to with training find direction, but to move to your destination you need to spend time to see where you are going before you even take a step. You cannot enjoy food if you cannot see it to determine its beauty and taste to your buds. Take the time to see what you want to do, what you want to become, and begin to believe God for it to happen.

Focus would also mean by reason of God's Word, declaring a positive result in the face of apparent lack.

So that when the doctor says you are barren, you rejoice because of your fruitfulness. When he says you would die because of the cancerous cells in your body, you proclaim you would not die but live to declare the glory of God.

Such focus on God's Word and on the purpose God has for your life seals your breakthrough, perfects your healing and confirms what God has already put in motion concerning your life. If the problem persists always remember the Bible method for defeating Satan. It is in humbling yourself, refusing to cry for Satan, refusing to complain. It is refusing to bow to him, refusing to come below the standard of God's Word that places you in a place where you command divine power and you receive divine access.

Start looking where Jesus said to look, so you can start to see the victory He already prepared. There is a prepared place for you in the programme of God, you enter and secure it by reason of total concentration on the will and purpose of God.

Satan of course will try to blur your focus and vision. Remember a blurred vision is the reason for an inaccurate and non-objective opinion of a situation. A blurred vision would mean a fuzzy picture.

Ask the Lord to illuminate, enlighten and magnify your eyes to see clearly and be led clearly. You cannot afford an image that is not clear or sure.

I counsel thee to buy of me gold tried in the fire, that thou mayest be rich; and white raiment, that thou mayest be clothed, and that the shame of thy nakedness do not appear; and anoint thine eyes with eyesalve, that thou mayest see.
Revelation 3:18 (KJV)

The eyes of your understanding being enlightened; that ye may know what is the hope of his calling, and what the riches of the glory of his inheritance in the saints,
Ephesians 1:18 (KJV)

And Elisha prayed, and said, LORD, I pray thee, open his eyes, that he may see. And the LORD opened the eyes of the young man; and he saw: and, behold, the mountain was full of horses and chariots of fire round about Elisha.
2 Kings 6:17 (KJV)

Sharpen your focus by removing all those who are likely to distract.

Abraham released Lot when he requested to depart from him. People like Lot will not allow you to see clearly. They are responsible for the beam that blocks your sight, the beam that causes bad focus and the lack of singleness of purpose.

And the LORD said unto Abram, after that Lot was separated from him, Lift up now thine eyes, and look from the place where thou art northward, and southward, and eastward, and westward:
Genesis 13:14 (KJV)

Through focus Elisha saw victory where his servant saw defeat.

You can change the scenario by the image in your spirit which you choose to emphasise and superimpose on what seems unchangeable.

And he said, Go and spy where he is, that I may send and fetch him. And it was told him, saying, Behold, he is in Dothan.
Therefore sent he thither horses, and chariots, and a great host: and they came by night, and compassed the city about.
And when the servant of the man of God was risen early, and gone forth, behold, an host compassed the city both with horses and chariots. And his servant said unto him, Alas, my master! how shall we do?
And he answered, Fear not: for they that be with us are more than they that be with them. And Elisha prayed, and said, LORD, I pray thee, open his eyes, that he may see. And the LORD opened the eyes of the young man; and he saw: and, behold, the mountain was full of horses and chariots of fire round about Elisha.
2 Kings 6:13-17 (KJV)

Focus on the picture of victory you see in your spirit, even if what appears in the natural is overwhelming.

God's Word would eventually prevail over any situation. The more you focus on God's Word, the greater the chance for it to prevail.

For this cause therefore have I called for you, to see you, and to speak with you: because that for the hope of Israel I am bound with this chain.
Acts 28:20 (KJV)

Isaiah was a prince who enjoyed the attention of King Uzziah. It seemed from scripture that the presence of the king distracted the young prince who was also a prophet from focusing on the Lord and getting the kind of results he should get. All Uzziahs must leave for you to maximise your life.

In the year that king Uzziah died I saw also the Lord sitting upon a throne, high and lifted up, and his train filled the temple.
Isaiah 6:1 (KJV)

Ask the Lord to open your eyes and show you your coming favour.

The breakthrough around the corner, the home He has prepared for you. The ministry you are about to come into, the life He has already called you to live. The business opportunity which will open for you, and how He plans to bring your loved ones to Himself.

*Call unto me, and I will answer thee, and shew thee great and mighty things,
which thou knowest not.*
Jeremiah 33:3 (KJV)

*Moreover, brethren, I would not that ye should be ignorant, how that all our
fathers were under the cloud, and all passed through the sea;*
1 Corinthians 10:1 (KJV)

Do what the Word says when it says to lift up your eyes.

It means to give God undivided attention. This is the time for
such focus because every answer you need, to every question
you would ever raise, whether about home, challenges, or needs
are all in the scriptures.

Finally cultivate the habit of seeing it before you talk it or do it,

before you move or react. It basically means by the time you are
taking steps, it is based on information received from the throne
of heaven, before it becomes obvious to everyone. This should
inform and instruct you to avoid all relationships and
associations that do not affirm your destiny and future. If you
want to see doors opening - start focusing.

CHAPTER THREE

BREAKING THE THOUGHT BARRIER

We quoted earlier William Blake who said "Man's desires are limited by his perceptions, no-one can desire what he has not perceived."

The ability to process his thought and execute it as an action is one of the greatest assets of mankind.

The mind is one of the most intricate computers made by God. A storehouse of information, a powerhouse for the gathering of ideas, a place where visions, dreams and great ideas are born.

Every human achievement which we see around us began as the thought on somebody's mind. Bridges, computers, aeroplanes, landing on the moon, submarines, the internet, etc. God crowned man with this ability to convert thoughts to action. In a nutshell we are surrounded by what is somebody's product by reason of thought.

You are also a product of your thought; at least a good chunk of what happens to you is what has gone through a process of reasoning in you.

Battles are won or lost, firstly in the realm of thought before the physical arena. It is safe to conclude that the temptation of Jesus must have taken place in the realm of thought, since we read of no place in scripture where Satan had a physical manifestation. Thoughts have such power that they make people who meet us ask, "What is on your mind?" Because what you have on your mind can almost be read on your face, before it becomes the action of your life. Paul presents to us the fact that Jesus went through a process of thought in deciding to die for mankind.

Let this mind be in you, which was also in Christ Jesus:
Who, being in the form of God, thought it not robbery to be equal with God:
But made himself of no reputation, and took upon him the form of a servant, and was made in the likeness of men:
And being found in fashion as a man, he humbled himself, and became obedient unto death, even the death of the cross.
Wherefore God also hath highly exalted him, and given him a name which is above every name:
That at the name of Jesus every knee should bow, of things in heaven, and

things in earth, and things under the earth;
And that every tongue should confess that Jesus Christ is Lord, to the glory
of God the Father.
Philippians 2:5-11 (KJV)

We have established how great a weapon of conquest, achievement, increase etc, the mind is.

Yet, the enemy of the soul sabotages human thoughts and turns them around against the person who is doing the thinking. It is like the disease of multiple sclerosis; certain cells of the body that are supposed to defend and protect the body, but because of some genetic misinformation, turn around to begin to fight against the body and scar it.

BARRIERS OF UNRENEWED THOUGHT

Let us consider the barriers of unrenewed thought. There are several elements of the barriers of such a mind.

1. A MIND THAT IS FILLED WITH ASSUMPTIONS WILL NOT MAKE PROGRESS.

Assumption certainly is the 'mother of mess-ups'. It is that state of mind in which we conclude that certain things are the way we thought they are or will be. Often times our conclusions are premature and based on inadequate information. Unrenewed minds have a tendency to believe that what it has assumed is true.

2. A FEARING MIND.

For God hath not given us the spirit of fear; but of power, and of love, and of a sound mind.
2 Timothy 1:7 (KJV)

Fear makes a big thing out of little things. Psychologists tell us eighty-five percent of the things we are afraid of never happen.

3. A WANDERING MIND.

Wherefore gird up the loins of your mind, be sober, and hope to the end for the grace that is to be brought unto you at the revelation of Jesus Christ;
1 Peter 1:13 (KJV)

A mind that wanders around will not co-ordinate its thought for its benefit, but rather is scattered and therefore taken advantage of.

4. A CONFUSED MIND.

If any of you lack wisdom, let him ask of God, that giveth to all men liberally, and upbraideth not; and it shall be given him.
But let him ask in faith, nothing wavering. For he that wavereth is like a wave of the sea driven with the wind and tossed.
For let not that man think that he shall receive any thing of the Lord. A double minded man is unstable in all his ways.
James 1:5-8 (KJV)

James describes this as being double minded. The word double minded is from the Greek *dipsuchos* suggesting having *'two souls'* or a split personality. When our thoughts are unrenewed it in effect becomes unstable and instead of achieving or making progress, we are perpetually between two minds, between two personalities and unable to conclude. Many have not made progress because the barrier of double mindedness has held them in bondage.

5. A DOUBTFUL MIND.

And he marvelled because of their unbelief. And he went round about the villages, teaching.
Mark 6:6 (KJV)

The element of doubt tends to ooze through the human mind, but a doubtful mind will fail to trust what God says. Whereas you can only rise and conquer and achieve by your thoughts. If your thoughts are sickly thoughts, you will produce sickly results.

6. AN ANXIOUS/WORRIED MIND.

Cease from anger, and forsake wrath: fret not thyself in any wise to do evil.
Psalms 37:8 (KJV)

Worry makes a big thing out of every little thing.

Worry misjudges situations and causes incredible problems for the person who is suffering from it. His thoughts become twisted and his judgements are not straight. Your future is paralysed or energised by your thoughts and therefore you cannot afford to be bound by an anxious or worried mind. You must understand that if your thoughts are bad, the fruit it will produce will be similar. You cannot snap out of a state of mind unless your mind becomes renewed through the Word of God.

7. A JUDGEMENTAL OR SUSPICIOUS MIND.

A person who suffers from a judgemental, cynical, suspicious mind finds himself bound also by envious thoughts.

This kind of process of thinking makes you a prisoner in your own body, unable to trust anyone. Taking too much of your own thinking which is already twisted, acting on it and therefore causing more confusion for yourself and for the people around you.

The subsequent result in life is that you are where you are today because of what you thought about before. Therefore if your thought is not taking you in the direction you really desire, you must check where it all went wrong. Your life inevitably moves in the direction of your greatest thought.

8. A PASSIVE MIND.

My people are destroyed for lack of knowledge: because thou hast rejected knowledge, I will also reject thee, that thou shalt be no priest to me: seeing thou hast forgotten the law of thy God, I will also forget thy children.
Hosea 4:6 (KJV)

Active minds produce active people. Whatever you are passive about does not open its treasure house to you. It is time to get busy with a mind full of God.

9. PRESUMPTION.

Presumption is the brother to assumption;

it also draws conclusions about people, places, things and events, misinforming the mind and causing an action that may be regretted in the future.

10. BELIEVING A LIE.

If anything would reveal an unrenewed thought or mind, it is the tendency to easily believe a lie.

Such minds become the workshop for the devil. A place where he can sell error. Your only victory is through the Word of God. The Word in you will reveal your character during crisis. A man who allows his mind to be indolent, full of wrath and self-deception cannot know victory. You get the product of the seed you sow. If your mind is corrupt the fruit will be. So for happiness, health and prosperity, a perpetual self-planting in the Word is necessary.

THE PROCESS OF THE RENEWAL OF THE MIND

There is a process for getting your mind to work again in order to destroy every barrier and enter and possess what belongs to you. Firstly you must think positive thoughts. It is not just positive thinking but 'faith thinking', it is by thinking faith thoughts and speaking faith words, that your heart is lifted from the valley of defeat into the realms of unlimited victory.

HAVE THE MIND OF CHRIST

Let this mind be in you, which was also in Christ Jesus:
Philippians 2:5 (KJV)

If your mind is after Christ it will definitely be positive. The mind of Christ is selfless, achieving, progressive and looks after other people without neglecting itself.

HAVE A POSITIVE OUTLOOK AND ATTITUDE

You can only rise and conquer and achieve by the thoughts you think.

You are what you think; your thoughts feed your behaviour and character. If a man imagines demons in the dark, he sees demons everywhere, he breaks sweat and his action is informed by what he thought about. Remember that in spite of lies, misunderstandings and a host of discouraging things, Jesus remained positive, keeping His testimony.

125

To keep a renewed mind, you must learn to imitate the Lord Jesus Christ. Because as a man continues to think, so is he.

For as he thinketh in his heart, so is he: Eat and drink, saith he to thee; but his heart is not with thee.
Proverbs 23:7 (KJV)

IDENTIFY YOUR POINT OF WEAKNESS AND OVERCOME IT.

Whatever has become the weakness of your mind must be overcome, the barrier must be brought down so that progress can be made. Refuse to be depressed because depression steals life from you.

Therefore is my spirit overwhelmed within me; my heart within me is desolate.
Psalms 143:4 (KJV)

Remember the good times you have had in your moments of weakness, tiredness and discouragement and meditate on His goodness.

I remember the days of old; I meditate on all thy works; I muse on the work of thy hands.
Psalms 143:5 (KJV)

CHOOSE TO PRAISE GOD.

I stretch forth my hands unto thee: my soul thirsteth after thee, as a thirsty land. Selah.
Psalms 143:6 (KJV)

It is this deliberate action of acknowledging God in all of your ways that brings victory to you.

After all the scripture says not to lean on your own understanding. A person who by his thoughts leans on his smartness will very soon find out that smartness does not break down the barrier. It is trusting in God that does it.

ASK GOD FOR HIS HELP

Hear me speedily, O LORD: my spirit faileth: hide not thy face from me, lest I be like unto them that go down into the pit.
Psalms 143:7 (KJV)

LISTEN TO THE VOICE OF THE LORD

Cause me to hear thy lovingkindness in the morning; for in thee do I trust: cause me to know the way wherein I should walk; for I lift up my soul unto thee.
Psalms 143:8 (KJV)

ASK FOR DELIVERANCE

Deliver me, O LORD, from mine enemies: I flee unto thee to hide me.
Psalms 143:9 (KJV)

You cannot do it yourself.

Will power would not set you free if you must break the barrier of your thoughts.

Some of the things that are besetting you and holding you have been with you from childhood. You need deliverance from above to be totally free. A man who will know joy and overcome the suffering or bondage which his mind has brought, must do it perpetually by the deliverance of the Lord.

SEEK FOR GOD'S WISDOM, KNOWLEDGE AND LEADING

Teach me to do thy will; for thou art my God: thy spirit is good; lead me into the land of uprightness.
Psalms 143:10 (KJV)

And when you find it, do not meditate on the enormity of the problem you face, but on the reality of the Word given to you, the Word of God which cannot fail.

KEEPING A RENEWED MIND OR THOUGHT

To break the barrier and keep it down, it is imperative that you recognise the place of the Word of God in the daily battle to keep your mind positively on God's Word.

(For the weapons of our warfare are not carnal, but mighty through God to the pulling down of strong holds;)
Casting down imaginations, and every high thing that exalteth itself against the knowledge of God, and bringing into captivity every thought to the obedience of Christ;
2 Corinthians 10:4-5 (KJV)

Images will attempt to form again that remind you of the barriers you used to know. Paul says to cast down those images.

BE GOD-MINDED

Thou wilt keep him in perfect peace, whose mind is stayed on thee: because he trusteth in thee.
Isaiah 26:3 (KJV)

When your focus is God the world will not forget you.

DELIGHT YOURSELF IN THE LORD

Delighting yourself in the Lord is absolutely important for you to be able to walk in victory.

In Judges chapter 7:1 when God would call Gideon; after all the various tests he had presented to the Lord. God gave Gideon a new self-concept, a new self-esteem, a sense of self-worth which was necessary for him to be able to confront the enemies whom he was ordained to overcome.

Though his army was small, his godly self-esteem and his godly self-concept helped him to realise that a man with God is more than a majority.

REMEMBER THE GOODNESS OF THE LORD

My soul shall be satisfied as with marrow and fatness; and my mouth shall praise thee with joyful lips: When I remember thee upon my bed, and meditate on thee in the night watches.
Psalms 63:5-6 (KJV)

This will keep the barriers down so that you are not meditating on what may or may not be, but on the goodness of God in the past.

129

SPEND TIME IN FELLOWSHIP WITH GOD

Nevertheless I tell you the truth; It is expedient for you that I go away: for if I go not away, the Comforter will not come unto you; but if I depart, I will send him unto you.
John 16:7 (KJV)

Intimacy is found in the place of fellowship; the closer you are to God, the more like Him you become. The more of His fullness you see and become, the more of His character you develop. These are necessary tools if you must break down barriers and also help others to become barrier breakers.

BE LOVE CONSCIOUS

And we have known and believed the love that God hath to us. God is love; and he that dwelleth in love dwelleth in God, and God in him.
1 John 4:16 (KJV)

REFUSE TO WALK IN FEAR

There is no fear in love; but perfect love casteth out fear: because fear hath torment. He that feareth is not made perfect in love.
1 John 4:18 (KJV)

Every barrier torn down in your life will be re-introduced by Satan; you must make a conscious effort to see that it is not re-erected. When you feel unloved remember your ordination is that of a king and priest.

And from Jesus Christ, who is the faithful witness, and the first begotten of the dead, and the prince of the kings of the earth. Unto him that loved us, and washed us from our sins in his own blood,
And hath made us kings and priests unto God and his Father; to him be glory and dominion for ever and ever. Amen.
Revelation 1:5-6 (KJV)

Therefore remind the enemy that your position is not determined by your feeling on a particular day, but who you are in God. Raise the concept you have of yourself. Your mind will always want to play a trick on you, but if you are very clear as to who you are by reason of your meditation in God's Word, then your mind will not become a barrier but a doorway.

MEDITATE ON THE WORD OF GOD

This book of the law shall not depart out of thy mouth; but thou shalt meditate therein day and night, that thou mayest observe to do according to all that is written therein: for then thou shalt make thy way prosperous, and then thou shalt have good success.
Joshua 1:8 (KJV)

What a man spends the time muttering, meditating, and thinking on is what he eventually become.

God told Joshua, by reason of the thought process which comes through a renewed mind achieved by the Word of God, success will be guaranteed. Enter the same realm with Joshua and have unlimited success.

Think big, if you do not you would remain small.

When you think small you limit God. Take the limits off God. Barrier breaking believers must recognise the barrier of smallness which the church has taught for a long time. Think differently, you do not have to do it the way everyone has always done it. It is your difference that marks you out for distinction, not your similarity. If God had wanted everyone to be similar He would not have created six billion people with a different genetic coding, facial voice and visual uniqueness.

HAVE AN EXHORTATIVE MIND

Or he that exhorteth, on exhortation: he that giveth, let him do it with simplicity; he that ruleth, with diligence; he that sheweth mercy, with cheerfulness.
Romans 12:8 (KJV)

DEVELOP A THANKFUL MIND

Enter into his gates with thanksgiving, and into his courts with praise: be thankful unto him, and bless his name.
Psalms 100:4 (KJV)

These are the days when everyone expresses their opinion, complaints, and criticisms or rather 'feedback', as today's politically correct society would say. But God wants the believer to do the exact opposite of what is popular, to give thanks when he could have complained.

HAVE YOUR MIND STAYED ON THE LORD

Thou wilt keep him in perfect peace, whose mind is stayed on thee: because he trusteth in thee.
Isaiah 26:3 (KJV)

This is the way to be kept in perfect peace and refuse to allow those barriers to rise again.

BE A PIONEER, REJECT A SETTLERS SPIRIT

Make God central to your daily activity. Refuse to sell yourself cheap, remember you are a person of quality. Keep your royal connection to mind at all times. Recognise the importance of your stewardship and walk in its reality. Do not be afraid to make a change where necessary. Do not allow yesterday's mistakes to stop tomorrow's miracles. Refuse to tie your future achievement and breakthroughs to the actions or inaction of other people. Recognise the season in which you are and enjoy the harvest which it delivers.

CHAPTER FOUR

BREAKING THE SOUND BARRIER

The ability to hear is one of the most unique parts of God's creatures. For man it is not just a tool for picking sounds, it is his major source for gathering information which he processes and in turn acts upon. What a person hears can affect how they act or react. While faith comes by hearing, doubt also comes by hearing.

> *So then faith cometh by hearing, and hearing by the word of God.*
> *Romans 10:17 (KJV)*

The scripture say the children of Israel did not enter into God's rest because of unbelief, and their unbelief was informed by what they were told of the giants that were in the land. The ear is a gateway to the mind, so that what the mind would process and send to the brain to disperse to every part of the body comes from the ears.

135

God speaks, human flesh speaks, the devil also wants to be heard. If anything, the believer must learn to develop the ability to discern who is speaking in order to inform his reaction to what he has heard. If the ears would be the source to communicate the sound that becomes a barrier or a door, one would have to choose what they hear.

What you hear also shapes what you see, since all these senses are connected.

It is important to know that the barriers which sound can cause is major. What you hear either opens doors or closes them. What you hear causes a chain of reaction in you to bless or to curse, to receive or reject. What you hear determines your perception of persons, places or things. What you hear is a product of your location. A person in the market place would hear a sound peculiar to it.

The scriptures give us a figure of about six hundred thousand men of fighting ability who left Egypt, the same number for the women and possibly more than that number for children and older people. All the adults who left Egypt did not reach Caanan because they received the evil report which their own leaders brought when they went to spy land.

And they told him, and said, We came unto the land whither thou sentest us, and surely it floweth with milk and honey; and this is the fruit of it. Nevertheless the people be strong that dwell in the land, and the cities are walled, and very great: and moreover we saw the children of Anak there.

The Amalekites dwell in the land of the south: and the Hittites, and the Jebusites, and the Amorites, dwell in the mountains: and the Canaanites dwell by the sea, and by the coast of Jordan.

And Caleb stilled the people before Moses, and said, Let us go up at once, and possess it; for we are well able to overcome it.

But the men that went up with him said, We be not able to go up against the people; for they are stronger than we.

And they brought up an evil report of the land which they had searched unto the children of Israel, saying, The land, through which we have gone to search it, is a land that eateth up the inhabitants thereof; and all the people that we saw in it are men of a great stature.

And there we saw the giants, the sons of Anak, which come of the giants: and we were in our own sight as grasshoppers, and so we were in their sight.

Numbers 13:27-33 (KJV)

And all the congregation lifted up their voice, and cried; and the people wept that night. And all the children of Israel murmured against Moses and against Aaron: and the whole congregation said unto them, Would God that we had died in the land of Egypt! or would God we had died in this wilderness! And wherefore hath the LORD brought us unto this land, to fall by the sword, that our wives and our children should be a prey? were it not better for us to return into Egypt? And they said one to another, Let us make a captain, and let us return into Egypt. Then Moses and Aaron fell on their faces before all the assembly of the congregation of the children of Israel. And Joshua the son of Nun, and Caleb the son of Jephunneh, which were of them that searched the land, rent their clothes:

And they spake unto all the company of the children of Israel, saying, The land, which we passed through to search it, is an exceeding good land.

If the LORD delight in us, then he will bring us into this land, and give it us; a land which floweth with milk and honey.

Only rebel not ye against the LORD, neither fear ye the people of the land; for they are bread for us: their defence is departed from them, and the LORD is with us: fear them not.

Numbers 14:1-9 (KJV)

HEARING PROBLEM

Breaking the sound barrier in the natural realm is important but it cannot be compared to the need to hear clearly in matters of the spirit. In order to hear clearly so that you receive what God has for you, some problems need to be dealt with. The first of them is:

1. SPIRITUAL DEAFNESS

When spiritual deafness takes hold of a man it oppresses him causing him not to hear the Lord,

and therefore not to be able to obey. Spiritual deafness will mean the enemy taking advantage so that when the Word goes out by the Lord, one is not hearing the mind of the Lord. If a favour is coming, if an attack of the enemy is also coming, there is no way to hear because the ear has not been opened to pick the message sent out.

When Caleb and Joshua stood up in the congregation of the people, the words spoken by the ten previous orators of evil had caused such spiritual deafness that the children of Israel were unable to discern the mind of the Lord.

2. STUBBORNESS

Just like a snake that will not listen to the voice of a charmer; when a man is spiritually deaf he is unable to hear the call of the Lord or His warning. The voice of the charmer is an Asian practice which made such men to be able, by certain pronouncements, to call out the poison released by the serpent. In the case of certain serpents that are said to be deaf, no matter how much the charmer tries, the poison would remain.

3. SEARED CONSCIENCE

When a person has a conscience too difficult to convict he is unable to hear the Lord or do the right thing.

> *Now the Spirit speaketh expressly, that in the latter times some shall depart from the faith, giving heed to seducing spirits, and doctrines of devils; Speaking lies in hypocrisy; having their conscience seared with a hot iron; 1 Timothy 4:1-2 (KJV)*

Even for the unsaved person the conscience becomes an antenna with which he can receive.

A conscience differentiates man from beasts.

In spite of his unsaved condition he is still able to express the milk of kindness or to feel a conviction for wrong, but when the ears of his conscience are seared he is unable to hear any warning that comes from God.

4. COUNSEL OF THE UNGODLY

The counsel of the ungodly, particularly in matters that relate to God, will lead a person out of God's will and it will distract if a person does not have his spiritual ears tuned to hear God. The three words used in Psalm 1:1,

> *Blessed is the man that walketh not in the counsel of the ungodly, nor standeth in the way of sinners, nor sitteth in the seat of the scornful.*
> *Psalms 1:1 (KJV)*

The *ungodly, sinners* and *scornful* reveal the fact that what you hear from such persons may stop you from receiving what God has for you.

'Ungodly' comes from the Hebrew *"rashal"* and means *'morally wrong, actively bad, wicked, unjust'*.

'Sinners' comes from *'chattal'* and means *'criminal, to miss the mark, to pass the limits of the law'*.

'Scornful' comes from *'luwts'* it means *'to make mouths at, to scuff, to mock'*. It is difficult to hear God if the source of a person's counsel is any of the three mentioned.

5. WRONG FREQUENCY

One more reason for the barriers to hearing God clearly is, if one is on the wrong frequency as compared to where God is operating. If you are not listening to God then you cannot hear. You would hear what you listen to. The children of Israel in the story earlier indicated were so busy listening to the evil report of the ten spies that they missed God's frequency and did not hear God at all.

6. BAD RECEPTION

Have you ever used a short-wave radio while you were driving? As you go further and further away from the area of operation where the frequency of the station is stronger, reception becomes bad and interference increases until the sound is replaced by static.

The same thing applies in the spirit realm. Many are not hearing what God wants them to hear, and what they are hearing is now becoming a barrier to them hearing God clearly. It has become a barrier to them hearing what God has in store for them. Unless those barriers are removed progress becomes difficult.

If you listen and pay close attention, the ear of your spirit will be opened and you would no longer be misdirected by the voices around you.

God spoke to Adam and Eve clearly, they knew His mind and what He wanted.

And the LORD God called unto Adam, and said unto him, Where art thou? And the LORD God said unto the woman, What is this that thou hast done? And the woman said, The serpent beguiled me, and I did eat.
Genesis 3:9, 13 (KJV)

Abraham was minding his own business when the voice of the Lord changed his destiny and introduced him to the favour and blessing earmarked for him.

Now the LORD had said unto Abram, Get thee out of thy country, and from thy kindred, and from thy father's house, unto a land that I will shew thee: And I will make of thee a great nation, and I will bless thee, and make thy name great; and thou shalt be a blessing: And I will bless them that bless thee, and curse him that curseth thee: and in thee shall all families of the earth be blessed.
Genesis 12:1-3 (KJV)

His friendship with God meant that God would do nothing unless He first showed it to His confidant.

And the LORD said, Shall I hide from Abraham that thing which I do;
Genesis 18:17 (KJV)

And he said, Oh let not the Lord be angry, and I will speak yet but this once: Peradventure ten shall be found there. And he said, I will not destroy it for ten's sake.
Genesis 18:32 (KJV)

When Moses went out taking care of sheep, he heard a voice that would turn his confusion and 'lostness' to direction and purpose. Holy men of God spoke as they were led of God because they had the ear that received from the Lord. Jesus describes the relationship of the sheep and the shepherd in the book of John.

On the hills of Palestine, five shepherds with a thousand sheep between them may all mix and graze together, but when it is evening and time for the shepherds to go home, all they need to do is make a peculiar sound, and by the sound of the shepherd each sheep will go back to its own fold.

To him the porter openeth; and the sheep hear his voice: and he calleth his own sheep by name, and leadeth them out.
And when he putteth forth his own sheep, he goeth before them, and the sheep follow him: for they know his voice.
And a stranger will they not follow, but will flee from him: for they know not the voice of strangers.
John 10:3-5 (KJV)

There is a dimension to our walk with God which requires the ear of our spirit to hear Him so we can rise and do spiritual and supernatural exploits, even the ones we did not expect.

And the Lord said unto him, Arise, and go into the street which is called Straight, and enquire in the house of Judas for one called Saul, of Tarsus: for, behold, he prayeth,
And hath seen in a vision a man named Ananias coming in, and putting his hand on him, that he might receive his sight.
Then Ananias answered, Lord, I have heard by many of this man, how much evil he hath done to thy saints at Jerusalem:
And here he hath authority from the chief priests to bind all that call on thy name.
But the Lord said unto him, Go thy way: for he is a chosen vessel unto me, to bear my name before the Gentiles, and kings, and the children of Israel:
For I will shew him how great things he must suffer for my name's sake.
Acts 9:11-16 (KJV)

Beloved, God is sounding out a message today, it is a clarion call of victory, favour, blessing and grace. It is time to get on God's frequency and hear Him clearly.

31 WAYS TO BREAK THE SOUND BARRIER

1. Circumcise your ears.

To whom shall I speak, and give warning, that they may hear? behold, their ear is uncircumcised, and they cannot hearken: behold, the word of the LORD is unto them a reproach; they have no delight in it.
Jeremiah 6:10 (KJV)

2. Hear His Word continuously and consistently.

Specially the day that thou stoodest before the LORD thy God in Horeb, when the LORD said unto me, Gather me the people together, and I will make them hear my words, that they may learn to fear me all the days that they shall live upon the earth, and that they may teach their children.
Deuteronomy 4:10 (KJV)

3. Form a habit of listening to God's divine instruction in order to discover and pursue His destiny to your life.

Observe and hear all these words which I command thee, that it may go well with thee, and with thy children after thee for ever, when thou doest that which is good and right in the sight of the LORD thy God.
Deuteronomy 12:28 (KJV)

4. Fill your heart with testimonies of joy and gladness, refuse to meditate on the negatives.

Awake up, my glory; awake, psaltery and harp: I myself will awake early.
Psalms 57:8 (KJV)

5. Meditate constantly on the words that can change your life.

For he is our God; and we are the people of his pasture, and the sheep of
his hand. To day if ye will hear his voice,
Harden not your heart, as in the provocation, and as in the day of
temptation in the wilderness:
Psalms 95:7-8 (KJV)

6. Read words that will increase your understanding of God regularly.

7. A wise man will hear, and will increase learning; and a man of understanding shall attain unto wise counsel.

8. To understand a proverb, and the interpretation; the words of the wise, and their dark sayings.

9. The fear of the LORD is the beginning of knowledge: but fools despise wisdom and instruction.

My son, hear the instruction of thy father, and forsake not the law of thy mother:
Proverbs 1:5-8 (KJV)

10. Listen to the rebuke of the wise so that the barriers which foolishness have created will fall.

It is better to hear the rebuke of the wise, than for a man to hear the song of fools.
Ecclesiastes 7:5 (KJV)

11. Listen to your loved ones regularly, do not be so far from them that you are not hearing their heart.

O my dove, that art in the clefts of the rock, in the secret places of the stairs, let me see thy countenance, let me hear thy voice; for sweet is thy voice, and thy countenance is comely.
Song of Solomon 2:14 (KJV)

12. Seek and listen to the voice of the Lord for clear direction on major and minor issues

And thine ears shall hear a word behind thee, saying, This is the way, walk ye in it, when ye turn to the right hand, and when ye turn to the left.
Isaiah 30:21 (KJV)

13. Build on what you hear within you, do not be led by what you see outside unless it is positive and confirming the Word of God.

While we look not at the things which are seen, but at the things which are not seen: for the things which are seen are temporal; but the things which are not seen are eternal.
2 Corinthians 4:18 (KJV)

14. Hear with the ear of the Spirit so that you can know the way of the Lord better.

Blessed is the man that heareth me, watching daily at my gates, waiting at the posts of my doors.
For whoso findeth me findeth life, and shall obtain favour of the LORD.
Proverbs 8:34-35 (KJV)

He that hath an ear, let him hear what the Spirit saith unto the churches; To him that overcometh will I give to eat of the tree of life, which is in the midst of the paradise of God.
Revelation 2:7 (KJV)

For verily I say unto you, That whosoever shall say unto this mountain, Be thou removed, and be thou cast into the sea; and shall not doubt in his heart, but shall believe that those things which he saith shall come to pass; he shall have whatsoever he saith.
Therefore I say unto you, What things soever ye desire, when ye pray, believe that ye receive them, and ye shall have them.
Mark 11:23-24 (KJV)

And Moses sent them to spy out the land of Canaan, and said unto them, Get you up this way southward, and go up into the mountain:
Numbers 13:17 (KJV)

But all the congregation bade stone them with stones. And the glory of the LORD appeared in the tabernacle of the congregation before all the children of Israel.
Numbers 14:10 (KJV)

15. Activate your hearing through the force of fasting and prayer.

Fasting and prayer have been mentioned in this book previously so we would not do an exhaustive teaching here. It is important to recognise that as you fast and pray it gives you the opportunity to silence your flesh and listen more to God. It raises your access to spiritual information, it keeps your attention on God and not on what your natural organs demand for.

The ear of our spirit is more attuned to God during periods of fasting because our point of concentration is hearing from God, or Him hearing from us. Our hearing can even be better as we study to be quiet until we hear the voice of the Lord.

16. Develop the ability to hear the sound of rain, even in the time of drought.

And Elijah said unto Ahab, Get thee up, eat and drink; for there is a sound of abundance of rain.
1 Kings 18:41 (KJV)

17. Hear the sound that says go ahead, fight and win even when it seems obvious in the natural that you will be defeated.

Consistently listen to the sound of worship and music, surround yourself with the high praise of God. By doing this you enthrone the Lord in His temple.

Thus all Israel brought up the ark of the covenant of the LORD with shouting, and with sound of the cornet, and with trumpets, and with cymbals, making a noise with psalteries and harps.
1 Chronicles 15:28 (KJV)

18. Be attentive to hear God so that other voices will not matter, because if you hear God the world will want to hear from you.

Hear attentively the noise of his voice, and the sound that goeth out of his mouth.
Job 37:2 (KJV)

19. Make a joyful sound yourself, speak the goodness of the Lord at all times.

Blessed is the people that know the joyful sound: they shall walk, O LORD, in the light of thy countenance.
Psalms 89:15 (KJV)

20. Train your ear to hear the sound of the Spirit so if others around you do not pick it, you are able to discern and know the mind of the Lord.

The wind bloweth where it listeth, and thou hearest the sound thereof, but canst not tell whence it cometh, and whither it goeth: so is every one that is born of the Spirit.
John 3:8 (KJV)

And suddenly there came a sound from heaven as of a rushing mighty wind, and it filled all the house where they were sitting.
Acts 2:2 (KJV)

21. Take time away from everything, make it a time you do not present a prayer request - just listen.

22. Listen to those who will inspire your vision, as you do so you are perpetually exposing yourself to the sounds that remove the barriers and turn themselves to the doorways to your favour and blessing.

23. Incline your ears to hear God alone in the midst of many voices.

I have called upon thee, for thou wilt hear me, O God: incline thine ear unto me, and hear my speech.
Psalms 17:6 (KJV)

My son, attend to my words; incline thine ear unto my sayings.
Proverbs 4:20 (KJV)

So that thou incline thine ear unto wisdom, and apply thine heart to understanding;
Proverbs 2:2 (KJV)

Incline your ear, and come unto me: hear, and your soul shall live; and I will make an everlasting covenant with you, even the sure mercies of David.
Isaiah 55:3 (KJV)

24. When you hear God speak to you obey His voice without delay.

Harden not your heart, as in the provocation, and as in the day of temptation in the wilderness:
Psalms 95:8 (KJV)

25. At a time of many choices learn to distinguish and obey the voice of the Lord.

Harden not your heart, as in the provocation, and as in the day of temptation in the wilderness:
Psalms 95:8 (KJV)

26. Develop your heart to be able to hear God even when your natural ears want to deceive you.

But as it is written, Eye hath not seen, nor ear heard, neither have entered into the heart of man, the things which God hath prepared for them that love him.
But God hath revealed them unto us by his Spirit: for the Spirit searcheth all things, yea, the deep things of God.
1 Corinthians 2:9-10 (KJV)

27. Reject and refuse every noise that wants to distract you from the purpose of God.

28. Remove the barriers to hearing from God.

Behold, the LORD'S hand is not shortened, that it cannot save; neither his ear heavy, that it cannot hear:
But your iniquities have separated between you and your God, and your sins have hid his face from you, that he will not hear.
Isaiah 59:1-2 (KJV)

29. Hear the Word and hear God, He has something to say to you.

Hear the word of the LORD, ye that tremble at his word; Your brethren that hated you, that cast you out for my name's sake, said, Let the LORD be glorified: but he shall appear to your joy, and they shall be ashamed.
Isaiah 66:5 (KJV)

30. Control what you hear, choose what you hear, challenge what you hear.

And Caleb stilled the people before Moses, and said, Let us go up at once, and possess it; for we are well able to overcome it.
Numbers 13:30 (KJV)

31. Change what you hear.

And Joshua the son of Nun, and Caleb the son of Jephunneh, which were of them that searched the land, rent their clothes:
And they spake unto all the company of the children of Israel, saying, The land, which we passed through to search it, is an exceeding good land.
If the LORD delight in us, then he will bring us into this land, and give it us; a land which floweth with milk and honey.
Only rebel not ye against the LORD, neither fear ye the people of the land; for they are bread for us: their defence is departed from them, and the LORD is with us: fear them not.
Numbers 14:6-9 (KJV)

CHAPTER FIVE

THE BARRIER BREAKER ANOINTING

As we bring our study of these barriers together it becomes apparent that the enemy's reason for sending them is to create hurdles of impossibility, challenges and impossible situations. We are confronted with footholds and strongholds which are meant to keep us perpetually in a cave of inability.

It is against these kinds of barriers that we must come with a power beyond the sky. We have the right to do this because like King Cyrus we have been deputised to bring the barriers down.

Thus saith the LORD to his anointed, to Cyrus, whose right hand I have holden, to subdue nations before him; and I will loose the loins of kings, to open before him the two leaved gates; and the gates shall not be shut; I will go before thee, and make the crooked places straight: I will break in pieces the gates of brass, and cut in sunder the bars of iron:
Isaiah 45:1-2 (KJV)

Potentially, you have victory over the barriers which the enemy brings, but practically it has to be established for it to take place.

THE NAME OF JESUS

You make your victory manifest by reason of your application of the Name of Jesus. God appeared over seven thousand times in the Old Testament by His holy Name Yahweh or Jehovah. He sealed every promise He made, every covenant He signed with His Name. That is, because His Name is not just a tag, it is the powerful, glorious, holy and righteous Name that reveals His person. It worked in the Old Testament, and under this better covenant it is even of greater consequence.

Moses called that Name as he stretched his rod against the mighty Red Sea, and the sea parted. He called that Name as he appealed to heaven, and heaven's bakery provided enough for millions every day. When the people were thirsty in an arid desert land and he smote the Rock in that Name, it gave them water.

When we call that Name, satan sees the exalted throne of God.

He also sees the empty tomb from where the bearer of the Name rose, and knows that at the mention of that Name he must bow. Barriers have to move when you use the Name against every attack which comes from the enemy.

Wherefore God also hath highly exalted him, and given him a name which is above every name: That at the name of Jesus every knee should bow, of things in heaven, and things in earth, and things under the earth; And that every tongue should confess that Jesus Christ is Lord, to the glory of God the Father.
Philippians 2:9-11 (KJV)

So confront and tear down the barrier with the Name.

THE ANOINTING

Recognise that you have the anointing of the Holy Spirit upon your life.

And grieve not the holy Spirit of God, whereby ye are sealed unto the day of redemption.
Ephesians 4:30 (KJV)

It shall come to pass in that day That his burden will be taken away from your shoulder, And his yoke from your neck, And the yoke will be destroyed because of the anointing oil.
Isaiah 20:27 (NKJV)

David said God anoints our head with oil.

Thou preparest a table before me in the presence of mine enemies: thou anointest my head with oil; my cup runneth over.
Psalms 23:5 (KJV)

The anointing puts a seal upon your life which demons cannot break through.

Satan himself cannot penetrate it and whatever barrier he has brought to stop you, he finds that the barriers must give way when the anointing oil is in operation.

The scriptures say every yoke will be destroyed, every burden will be removed. By reason of the anointing your salvation cannot be stolen, your healing cannot be taken, what God has given you remains with you.

157

The anointing of the Holy Spirit becomes your seal and sign that you are God's property and therefore the enemy must beware. That seal goes with you everywhere, when you are lost like the prodigal son, that seal brings you home. When you are confronted with problems, the Spirit of the Lord will raise a standard against it.

When people want to deceive you and pressurise you into doing their own thing, the anointing of the Holy Spirit will be there to give you the boldness to say no without feeling guilty.

It is this power of the Holy Spirit that would help you to tear down what the enemy means to hold you with.

THE BLOOD OF JESUS

The third barrier breaker is the blood.

And they shall take of the blood, and strike it on the two side posts and on the upper door post of the houses, wherein they shall eat it.

For I will pass through the land of Egypt this night, and will smite all the firstborn in the land of Egypt, both man and beast; and against all the gods of Egypt I will execute judgment: I am the LORD.
And the blood shall be to you for a token upon the houses where ye are: and when I see the blood, I will pass over you, and the plague shall not be upon you to destroy you, when I smite the land of Egypt.
Exodus 12:7, 12, 13 (KJV)

The author of Hebrews says that the blood of Jesus speaks better things, and one of the things it speaks is victory against every barrier.

And to Jesus the mediator of the new covenant, and to the blood of sprinkling, that speaketh better things than that of Abel.
Hebrews 12:24 (KJV)

It is the blood which ratifies and authenticates. It is the blood which protects and keeps you from falling. That blood went with Paul to the island of Melita. The bite of the snake was not effective on him. That blood was used in heaven to fight against satan, the dragon and his hosts.

And they overcame him by the blood of the Lamb, and by the word of their
testimony; and they loved not their lives unto the death.
Revelation 12:11 (KJV)

It is a barrier breaking blood that will tear down the weapons of the enemy. It is also able to seal you from the encroachment of death as we see in the exodus of the children of Israel from Egypt. It becomes a covering on your household.

So the destroyer cannot touch what belongs to you. Satan cannot steal your healing or come near your dwelling place.

The barrier breaker anointing we are told will tear down the bars of iron and come against every gate of brass.

You are unstoppable by reason of the barrier breaker anointing.

I will go before thee, and make the crooked places straight: I will break in
pieces the gates of brass, and cut in sunder the bars of iron:
Isaiah 45:2 (KJV)

And when in the end you have your victory, you will be able to say like David:

Oh that men would praise the LORD for his goodness, and for his wonderful
works to the children of men!
For he hath broken the gates of brass, and cut the bars of iron in sunder.
Psalms 107:15-16 (KJV)